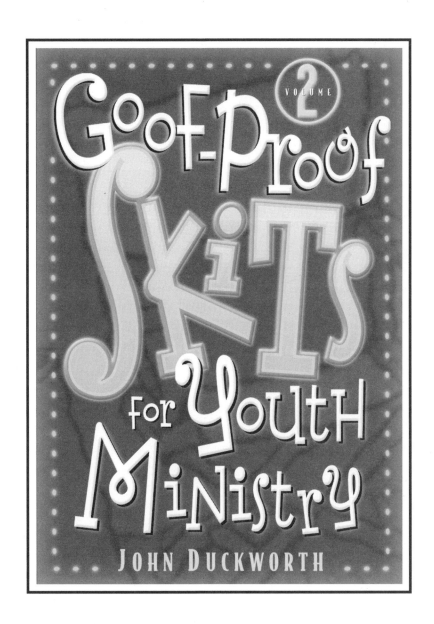

VOLUME 2

Goof-Proof Skits for Youth Ministry

John Duckworth

Group

Loveland, Colorado

Dedication

To Dad, with thanks for the theater gene—
and to Mom, with thanks for the writing chromosome.

Goof-Proof Skits for Youth Ministry 2
Copyright © 2000 John Duckworth

Visit our Web site: **www.grouppublishing.com**

CREDITS
Book Acquisitions Editor: Amy Simpson
Editor: Michael D. Warden
Creative Development Editor: Jim Kochenburger
Chief Creative Officer: Joani Schultz
Copy Editor: Alison Imbriaco
Art Director: Jean Bruns
Designers: Helen Lannis, Jean Bruns
Computer Graphic Artist: Joyce Douglas
Cover Art Director: Jeff A. Storm
Cover Designer: Rick Dembicki
Production Manager: Alexander Jorgensen

Unless otherwise noted, Scripture taken from the HOLY BIBLE, NEW INTERNA-TIONAL VERSION. Copyright © 1973, 1978, 1984 by International Bible Society. Used by permission of Zondervan Publishing House. All rights reserved.

Library of Congress Cataloging-in-Publication Data
Duckworth, John (John L.)
   Goof-proof skits for youth ministry / by John Duckworth.
        p.   cm.
     Includes indexes.
   ISBN 1-55945-795-3 (v. 1)
   ISBN 0-7644-2142-5 (v. 2)
      1. Drama in Christian education. 2. Church work with teenagers. 3. Amateur plays. I. Title.
   BV1534.4.D289   1995
   246'.7–dc20   95-17207
                                                                    CIP

10 9 8 7 6 5 4 3 2 1   09 08 07 06 05 04 03 02 01 00
Printed in the United States of America.

1.00

Contents

Goof-Proof Skits for Youth Ministry 2

Introduction

Welcome to a Skit Book for <u>Every</u> Group!

Sure, skits are a great idea for youth ministry. They can make learning active and visual. They build relationships as kids learn to work together. They brighten meetings with humor while driving home important points.

But only if your kids can *act*.

If your group is like most—that is, if it's not composed entirely of drama-club presidents and speech-team captains—your experiences with skits may be nothing to write home about. If some of your kids are "theatrically challenged," you may find yourself avoiding skits entirely or using the same few talented kids again and again.

Your dilemma: Should you keep less skilled members of your group off the stage, making them feel left out? Or should you use everybody and limp through some ineffective and embarrassing efforts?

There's a better way, you know—goof-proof skits. First there was the popular *Goof-Proof Skits for Youth Ministry*. And now, to keep your store of sure-fire scripts full, here's volume 2!

Real Fun, Real Truths—for Real Kids.

What do you want in a skit? Fun? It's here—from pratfalls to parables to TV show parodies. Solid, Bible-based messages? They're here, too—on important topics, including decision-making, violence, and inviting others to the group.

But you get more than sound messages and plenty of fun with *Goof-Proof Skits for Youth Ministry* 2. You get help to make each skit work.

Every script in this book has been prepared with real kids in mind. You'll find no page-long speeches to stumble through, no delicate emotional nuances to steamroll, no split-second timing to fumble. The language is simple, and the feelings are straightforward.

Best of all, *Goof-Proof Skits for Youth Ministry* 2 gives you innovative cues to help you draw the best possible reading—and the most meaning—from every line of dialogue. Every script provides simple facial-expression symbols to show kids instantly how to put the right feeling into each line. To help beat the "monotone syndrome" and ensure that everyone catches key concepts, words that should be spoken with emphasis are set in capital letters.

The result? Skits that build confidence. Skits that let you cast practically anybody. Skits that cut mistakes to a minimum so that the message can't miss. Skits that work in any group—dramatically inclined or not.

Goof-Proof Skits for Youth Ministry 2 may not turn your kids into Tony award winners. But when it comes to getting all your kids involved—and getting the message across ungarbled—you'll find no better or easier way than with this series of resources.

Use this book in your youth meetings, retreats, Sunday school, Bible studies, or worship services—with or without rehearsal—whenever you want to make a point in a fresh, funny, memorable way. With each script, you'll find Scriptures to study, a relevant topic to explore, easy setup ideas, thought-provoking discussion questions, and optional extras. You'll find so much, in fact, that you can turn each skit into a complete youth group session of its own—if you want to.

And After the Skit?

Youth ministry doesn't end when the skit's over—so the skits in this book don't end there either. You can take advantage of the discussion questions in the "For Post-Play Pondering" section to help your kids dig deeper into the skit topics.

As you lead kids in post-play pondering, remember that variety and interaction help make discussions exciting for teenagers. Use large groups, small groups, pairs, and trios. Or have kids number off from one to five, then have all the ones respond to the first question, all the twos respond to the second, and so on. Or have kids write their own questions about the topic based on what they saw in the skit. The possibilities are almost endless!

A great skit can be one of your most powerful tools for helping teenagers grow in faith— if it works. The goof-proof skits and post-play ponderings in this book are your chance to get more of that dramatic power off the page—and into the hearts of your group members.

Key to Expression Symbols

To help group members know at a glance how to say their lines, the dialogue in this book includes simple facial-expression symbols. Most kids will grasp quickly the emotions represented by the symbols, so you shouldn't need to explain them. For *your* reference, though, here are the *official* meanings of those little faces.

Calm, Pleasant	Puzzled, Unsure, Thinking
Happy, Hopeful	Sarcastic, Skeptical
Laughing	Mumbling, Whispering
Relieved	Bored, Disinterested
Serious, Earnest	Slick, Phony
Smug, Boastful, Condescending	Sheepish, Embarrassed
Shy, Innocent	Proud, Haughty
Nervous, Worried	Crying
Scared	Excited
Surprised, Shocked	Sick, Disoriented, Tired
Screaming, Hysterical	Emotionless
Malicious, Sneaky	Crazy, Goofy
Disgusted	Angry
Irritated, Complaining	Pained, Strained
Sad, Depressed, Sorry	Hypnotized, Zombielike

Bratman

Topic: Serving God While You're Young

Scripture for Study:
Ecclesiastes 12:1-7

The Scene: The sitting room of a mansion

The Simple Setup: For this spoof of the *Batman* movies and TV series, place one chair near center stage, facing stage left. For props use a comic book, headphones, a bag of chips, and a cordless telephone. Note that **Bratman** and **Boy Whiner** do not wear superhero costumes; school clothes are fine. If possible, the actor playing **Albert** should be older (or made up to look older) and should try for a British accent. **Albert** should wear a dark suit—one an offstage helper can mess up and even tear in a few seconds. (See script; if you can't damage the suit, take off the jacket during the offstage change and replace it with a torn one, or simply mess up the shirt and tie).

Other Options: If you can, play a little of the opening theme music from one of the *Batman* movie soundtracks to lead into the skit.

The Characters:

    Bratman, selfish crime-fighter
    The Boy Whiner, annoying sidekick
    Albert, elderly and long-suffering butler

*(As the skit begins, **Bratman** and **Boy Whiner** lounge center stage. Both are "out of uniform" in school clothes. **Bratman** sits on a chair, reading a comic book; **Boy Whiner** sits on the floor, eating chips from a bag, wearing headphones, and bopping up and down as if to music. After a few moments, **Albert** enters, carrying a cordless phone.)*

Albert:		(To **Bratman**) It's…the BRAT-PHONE, sir.
Bratman:		The BRAT-PHONE? Not NOW, Albert! I'm just getting to the GOOD PART in this COMIC BOOK!
Albert:		But, SIR…it's COMMISSIONER CORKGUN. He says he's been shining the BRAT-SIGNAL in the sky for HOURS, trying to get your ATTENTION.
Bratman:		WHAT, am I supposed to STARE OUT THE WINDOW all the time in case he decides to SHINE that thing? I've got a LIFE, you know!
Albert:		Sir…he says it's URGENT.
Bratman:		(*Grabbing phone; to **Albert***) Oh, it's ALWAYS urgent. Always some guy in a STUPID COSTUME threatening FLOTSAM CITY. Why do they keep calling

ME? What do we pay these POLICEMEN for? (*Speaking into phone*) This is BRATMAN! (*Pauses.*) YES, Commissioner. (*Pauses.*) Well, I was just sitting here in my STATELY MANOR, along with my SIDEKICK, the BOY WHINER, doing some important…RESEARCH. (*Pauses.*) WHO'S back? The CHOKER? He wants to TAKE OVER Flotsam City by pumping the ART MUSEUM full of LAUGHING GAS, STEALING the MOPE DIAMOND, and holding it for RANSOM? (*Rolls his eyes.*) WHATEVER. (*Pauses.*) YEAH, yeah. We'll get right ON it. (*Gives phone to **Albert**, then turns to **Boy Whiner**.*) HEY, Boy Whiner!

(**Boy Whiner** *continues to listen to music and eat chips.*)

Bratman: I'm TALKING to you!

(**Boy Whiner** *ignores him.* **Bratman** *yanks off headphones.*)

Boy Whiner: OW! I was LISTENING to that, you big BULLY!

Bratman: Time for ACTION! The CHOKER is on the loose!

Boy Whiner: The CHOKER! Why, that means…

Bratman: RIGHT! It means we have to… SEND ALBERT!

Albert: But, SIR…

Bratman: Quit WHINING, Albert.

Boy Whiner: YEAH, Albert. You can't expect US to go out crime-fighting. We're too YOUNG to worry about that stuff.

Albert: But I'm just an old BUTLER, sir…

Bratman: So you're EXPERIENCED! We're NOT!

Boy Whiner: And we don't WANT to be, so don't try to TEACH us anything!

Albert: But I can't even LIFT the PROTECTIVE BODY ARMOR…

Bratman: Aw, YOU don't want to wear THAT ANYWAY. It just makes you SWEATY, and then you SMELL UP my STATELY MANOR.

(**Bratman** *and* **Boy Whiner** *start pushing* **Albert** *offstage.*)

Albert: But how will I DEFEAT the CHOKER?

Bratman: You'll think of SOMETHING. Have a NICE TIME!

(**Bratman** and **Boy Whiner** push **Albert** offstage, then return to their lounging.)

Boy Whiner: The NERVE of that Albert! Always trying to get US to fight the bad guys!

Bratman: YEAH! Doesn't he know that stuff's for OLD people?

(For a few moments, **Bratman** reads his comic book and **Boy Whiner** eats chips. Suddenly a bedraggled **Albert**, his clothes looking torn and dirty, stumbles in, panting. He is carrying the phone.)

Bratman: ALBERT! Back ALREADY?

Albert: YES…sir…

Boy Whiner: Did you BEAT the CHOKER?

Albert: I…THINK so…sir…

Bratman: And did you remember to WASH the BRAT-MOBILE before returning it to the BRAT-CAVE?

Albert: (Falling to his hands and knees) Yes…sir…

Boy Whiner: Pretty GOOD for an OLD guy! Take FIVE, Albert. Oh, but get me some more CHIPS first, will ya?

(**Albert** starts to crawl offstage, then makes a phone ringing sound, and crawls back to the phone.)

Albert: (Offering phone to **Bratman**) It's…the BRAT-PHONE, sir…

(**Bratman** takes phone; **Albert** collapses on the floor.)

Bratman: (To **Boy Whiner**) I guess Commissioner CORKGUN wants to CONGRATU-LATE us. (Speaking into phone) YES, Commissioner. (Pauses.) WHAT? You say three MORE supervillains have BANDED TOGETHER? The FIDDLER…RATWOMAN…and MR. SLEAZE? They want to TAKE OVER Flotsam City by HYPNOTIZING everyone with a giant RAY GUN, then ROBBING all the BANKS and putting EXTRA FAT in the DRINKING WATER? (Rolls eyes.) WHATEVER. Yeah, we'll take CARE of it. (To **Albert**) Hey, ALBERT! Looks like you've got more WORK to do!

(**Albert** lies motionless.)

Bratman: ALBERT!

Boy Whiner: Come ON, Albert! Don't just LIE there! Get MOVING!

(**Bratman** *takes* **Albert's** *pulse.*)

Bratman: He...he's DEAD!

Boy Whiner: Oh, GREAT! Now who's going to get my CHIPS?

Bratman: It's worse than THAT. Who's going to save Flotsam City from the ARCH CRIMINALS who've JOINED FORCES to DESTROY it?

Boy Whiner: Not US! We're too YOUNG! Let's not think about that stuff until we're OLD!

Bratman: (*Looking into the distance*) You know, Boy Whiner...I've been THINKING. Maybe Albert was RIGHT. Maybe it IS time for the NEXT GENERATION to start doing its PART. Maybe it's time to LEARN from those who are OLDER, to add the STRENGTH of YOUTH, to stop putting off RESPONSI-BILITY and begin to CHANGE THE WORLD before it's too LATE. (*Pauses.*) Yes...this is a job for...BRATGIRL!

Boy Whiner: Yeah! BRATGIRL! She's at least a MONTH OLDER than I am! Let HER do the work!

Bratman: RIGHT! (*Dials phone as he starts to leave;* **Boy Whiner** *follows.*) Now, what WAS her NUMBER? (*They exit.*)

For Post-Play Pondering:

1. What reasons did Bratman and the Boy Whiner give for not fighting crime themselves? How are these reasons like the reasons some kids give for leaving "religious stuff" to older people?

2. Which of the following are you most likely to hear: (a) "I'm not old enough to stay up late"; (b) "I'm not old enough to be trusted with the car"; (c) "I'm not old enough to worry about that God stuff"? Why?

3. Is there a "right" age for getting serious about God? How do you know?

4. What are three things a teenager might be able to do for God that an adult probably couldn't?

5. What's one thing you'd like to learn about God? Which adult at church might be able to help you with that? How could you ask that person to help you this week?

Other Scriptures for Study:

Psalm 119:9-16; Acts 2:17; 1 Timothy 4:12

No Sweat

Topic: Stress

Scripture for Study:
Psalm 55

The Scene: Outside a school

The Simple Setup: You'll need a chair center stage, facing the audience. Roles may be played by either gender; actors may wear casual clothes. For props, have a geometry book, or a book with a paper cover labeled "Geometry," for **Kid** and a head-size paper bag for **Friend 1.**

Other Options: If possible, ask the person who plays **Kid** to practice the twitching, shaking, and blinking called for in the script; a little rehearsal of these "bits" and their timing will make them more effective.

The Characters:

> **Kid**, a stressed-out Christian
> **Friend 1**, a normal non-Christian
> **Friend 2**, another normal non-Christian

▼ ▼ ▼ ▼ ▼ ▼ ▼ ▼

*(As the skit begins, **Kid** is sitting on a chair center stage, facing the audience, studying the "Geometry" book.)*

Kid: This GEOMETRY! I just can't GET it! I'll NEVER get it! I'm gonna FLUNK OUT and MISS COLLEGE and NEVER GET A DECENT JOB! I'll end up having to be...a YOUTH PASTOR or something! *(Holds hand over heart, breathes quickly.)* I'm so STRESSED OUT! My PALMS are all SWEATY! *(Puts down book, wipes hands on pants.)* Maybe I'm gonna have a STROKE! *(Holds head.)*

*(Enter **Friends 1** and **2**, pantomiming a conversation.)*

Kid: Oh, NO! It's my NON-CHRISTIAN FRIENDS! I've got to stop being STRESSED OUT. If they SEE me like this, they'll NEVER want to be CHRISTIANS! I've got to get myself under CONTROL! *(Folds hands in lap and breathes deeply, trying to calm down.)* THAT'S it...breathe DEEPLY...everything's FINE...

Friend 1: *(To **Kid**)* HEY! How ya DOIN'?

Friend 2: *(Picking up book)* What are you STUDYING? WHOA! GEOMETRY! Man, THERE'S a subject that STRESSES ME OUT!

Friend 1: Me, TOO!

Friend 2: I mean, HOW am I supposed to remember the DIFFERENCE between a TRAPEZOID and a PARALLELOGRAM?

Friend 1: Or a CIRCLE and a SQUARE?

(**Kid** and **Friend 2** *frown.*)

Friend 1: Well, maybe THAT'S not so hard.

Friend 2: (*Putting book down*) Geometry ties my STOMACH up in KNOTS!

(**Kid** *winces and puts hand over own stomach.*)

Friend 1: It makes all the MUSCLES in my NECK TENSE!

(**Kid** *feels back of own neck and grimaces in pain.*)

Friend 2: (*To* **Kid**) So how do you DO it? How do you study GEOMETRY without turning into a BASKET CASE?

Kid: (*Folds hands in lap again and tries to look relaxed.*) It's…NOTHING…when you're…a CHRISTIAN.

Friend 1: REALLY?

Kid: SURE! I just…give all my problems to the LORD. Then it's SMOOTH SAILING! (**Kid's** *leg suddenly starts to shake violently.* **Kid** *clamps a hand on it, trying to hide the shaking.*)

Friend 2: (*Pointing at leg*) Hey, what's THAT?

Kid: Uh…NOTHING! Nothing at all! (*Leg keeps shaking.*)

Friend 1: So being a CHRISTIAN keeps you from going off the DEEP END, huh?

Kid: RIGHT! NO TROUBLES! (*One of* **Kid's** *eyes starts twitching and blinking vigorously as leg keeps shaking.*)

Friend 2: 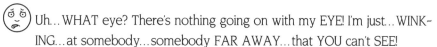 Uh…what's with your EYE?

Kid: Uh…WHAT eye? There's nothing going on with my EYE! I'm just…WINKING…at somebody…somebody FAR AWAY…that YOU can't SEE!

Friend 1:  HUH. Then being a CHRISTIAN GUARANTEES that the PRESSURE won't GET to you?

Kid: (*Still blinking and shaking*) You GOT it! I'm as cool as a CUCUMBER! (***Kid's*** *entire body begins to twitch uncontrollably.* ***Kid*** *tries in vain to get hold of self.*)

Friend 2: Are you...OK?

Kid: (*Forcing self to stay still.*) NEVER...BEEN...BETTER! (*Shaking and blinking again, with added outbursts of yelling.*) AAGGHH! It is WELL with my SOUL! YAAUUGGHH! I bet you wish YOU had the same INNER PEACE that I have! AAAUUUGGGHHH!

Friend 1: Uh...maybe you're HYPERVENTILATING. HERE, put my LUNCH BAG over your head and take DEEP BREATHS. (*Puts paper bag over* ***Kid's*** *head.* ***Kid*** *holds bag, takes a few deep breaths.*)

Kid: (*From inside the bag*) YUCK! What did you have for LUNCH?

Friend 1: SARDINE and LIMBURGER SANDWICH. SORRY.

(***Kid*** *takes a few more deep breaths and begins to calm down. Takes bag off.*)

Kid: (*Breathless*) SO...ah...do you want to...BECOME CHRISTIANS now? And have...the BLESSED ASSURANCE I have...in the STORM-TOSSED SEAS of LIFE?

Friend 2: Uh...NOT TODAY, thanks.

Friend 1: YEAH. Maybe ANOTHER time.

Kid: But you need...this UNFAILING STRENGTH...to face the STRAINS of LIVING!

Friend 2: Uh-HUH. See you AROUND.

Friend 1: You can KEEP the BAG. I have a feeling you're gonna NEED it. (***Friends*** *exit.*)

Kid: (*After a pause*) So...THAT went well! (*Picks up book and begins reading it while moving toward exit.*) UH-oh...MATHEMATICAL PROOFS! If A equals B...I mean, if D equals E... Oh, NO! I'll NEVER get this! (*Puts bag over head, starts breathing hard, and exits.*)

For Post-Play Pondering:

1. Which would stress you out most: (a) taking Scholastic Aptitude Tests, (b) acting in a school play, (c) taking the driver's-license road test, or (d) being fired from an after-school job? Why?

2. How can you tell when you're really stressed? How can others tell?

3. Do you think Christians should handle stress better than non-Christians do? Why or why not?

4. When you became a Christian—assuming you have—did you think that following Jesus would mean you'd have fewer problems? How do you feel about that now?

5. What advice would you give to the Christian in the skit? Why?

Other Scriptures for Study:

Psalm 62:1-8; Matthew 11:28-30; 1 Peter 5:7

Suddenly Stupid

The Scene: A dinner table

The Simple Setup: Put a table center stage; place four chairs around it. Set the table with plates, glasses, utensils, and food (torn-up bread will do); put water in the glasses. For props use a small bottle (a trial-size mouthwash bottle would work well) with water in it for **Brother** and a serving bowl for **Mom.** All actors may wear casual clothes.

Other Options: If you want to go the extra mile, add costumes (such as an apron for **Mom** and cardigan sweater for **Dad**) and makeup (eyeliner wrinkles and cornstarch on the hair, for example) that make the parents look older.

The Characters:

Brother, exasperated fifteen-year-old
Sister, much like **Brother**
Mom, patient but firm
Dad, much like **Mom**

▼ ▼ ▼ ▼ ▼ ▼ ▼ ▼

(As the skit begins, all the characters sit around a table as if eating dinner.)

Dad: I'm SORRY, Son. But this new SPORT you want to try sounds too DANGEROUS!

Brother: But, DAD…EVERYBODY'S going ROCK-SAILING!

Mom: ROCK-SAILING? What's THAT?

Brother: It's easy! You CLIMB up the side of a CLIFF using only TOILET PLUNGERS. When you get to the TOP, you hold a PAPER AIRPLANE in each hand and FALL BACKWARD, hoping the WIND will catch you!

Dad: I'm afraid we can't let you DO that, son.

Brother: WHAT? You never let me do ANYTHING!

Sister: That REMINDS me, Mom. Give me FIVE HUNDRED BUCKS, OK?

Mom: FIVE HUNDRED DOLLARS? What FOR?

Sister: Well, I'm going OUT with this guy SHAWN tomorrow night.

Dad: And?

Sister: I have to BAIL HIM OUT OF JAIL first.

Dad: JAIL? What kind of boy IS this Shawn?

Sister: He's really COOL. He's been on TV!

Mom: OH? Which SHOWS?

Sister: Um… COPS…AMERICA'S MOST WANTED…and WORLD'S SCARIEST POLICE CHASES.

Mom: I'm afraid we can't let you go OUT with this boy, dear.

Sister: WHAT? You never let me do ANYTHING!

Mom: (Sighing) I…think I'll go get more POTATOES. (Stands.)

Dad: I'll give you a HAND. (**Mom** and **Dad** exit.)

Sister: Mom and Dad drive me CRAZY! They never let us do ANYTHING!

Brother: Yeah, I KNOW. But I've got the SOLUTION.

Sister: WHAT?

Brother: (Takes a small bottle from his pocket and holds it up.) DUMB DROPS!

Sister: DUMB DROPS? What's THAT?

Brother: I got it from a kid at SCHOOL. He makes the stuff in his BASEMENT.

Sister: How does it WORK?

Brother: We just put a little in their WATER, and when they DRINK it, they turn…DUMB! So dumb they'll let us do ANYTHING!

Sister: REALLY? Let's TRY it—before they come BACK!

(**Brother** puts a few drops from the bottle into **Mom's** and **Dad's** water glasses and sits down. **Mom** and **Dad** enter; **Mom** carries a serving bowl. They sit.)

Mom: More POTATOES?

Brother: NO, thanks.

(**Brother** and **Sister** *stare at* **Mom** *and* **Dad**.)

Dad: Uh...why are you STARING at us?

Sister: STARING? WE'RE not staring!

Brother: We just...thought you'd like some WATER.

Sister: YEAH. You look really...

Brother: THIRSTY.

Dad: Well, I guess I AM a little PARCHED.

Mom: Me, TOO.

(**Mom** *and* **Dad** *each take a long drink of water, then put the glasses down.*)

Brother: SO...how do you FEEL?

Dad: FINE. Why do you...(**Dad** *suddenly sits up straight and bugs out his eyes.*)

Mom: Dear, are you all...(**Mom** *suddenly sits up straight and bugs out her eyes, too.*)

Brother: Uh...DAD...what's TWELVE TIMES SEVEN?

Dad: THREE!

Sister: MOM, where do you want to go on VACATION this year?

Mom: The SEWAGE TREATMENT PLANT!

Brother: (*To* **Sister**) It WORKS! They're...SUDDENLY STUPID!

Sister: (*To* **Mom** *and* **Dad**) SO, can I have that FIVE HUNDRED BUCKS to bail SHAWN out of JAIL?

Dad: You sure five hundred is ENOUGH? Big bank have MANY MONEYS!

Sister: Oh, GOOD! But let's START with five hundred.

Brother: And can I go ROCK-SAILING?

Mom: OOOH, pretty ROCKS! Go sail rocks, YES!

Brother: (*To* **Sister**) This is GREAT! They're so DUMB they'll let us do ANYTHING WE WANT!

Sister: (To **Brother**) Let's see what ELSE we can get. (To parents) While we're AT it, can I DROP OUT OF SCHOOL and spend a year AIRBRUSHING MY FINGERNAILS in FRANCE?

Mom: Oooh, PRETTY FINGERNAILS! Yes, YES! Have FRENCH FRIES, too!

Brother: Can I FILL MY ROOM with ONE HUNDRED THOUSAND WATTS of STEREO SPEAKERS...and dig a POISONOUS SNAKE PIT in the BACK-YARD?

Dad: Good IDEA! Loud music NICE! Poison snakes very FUN!

Sister: (To **Brother**) I can't BELIEVE this! How LONG do Dumb Drops LAST?

Brother: (To **Sister**) FOREVER, I guess! (To parents) Well, we need to go BUY some stuff, like JUNK FOOD and PLANE TICKETS. Could you DRIVE us to the MALL?

Dad: (Making steering motions) DRIVE! Brrrumm, BRRUMMM! Make car go FAST!

Mom: ME drive car! Go HUNDRED MILES AN HOUR!

Brother: (To **Sister**) UH-oh. They're too DUMB to DRIVE! We don't have our LICENSES yet! How will we GET anywhere?

Sister: I don't KNOW...but at least we can get some MONEY out of them! (To parents) OK...how about writing us a nice, big CHECK?

Dad: Me no can sign NAME!

Mom: Me NEITHER! (**Mom** and **Dad** look at each other and make goofy faces.)

Sister: (To **Brother**) NOW look what you've done! They're too STUPID to write a CHECK! They're too stupid to GO TO WORK and earn MONEY for us to SPEND!

Brother: They're too stupid to DRIVE US AROUND! Too stupid to COOK OUR MEALS! They're too stupid to do ANYTHING!

Sister: (Shaking **Brother**) DUMB DROPS? You must have swallowed a whole BOTTLE! (**Brother** runs out; **Sister** chases him.)

Mom: What he TALKING about? ME not too stupid to COOK!

Dad: Oh, GOOD! What we have for DESSERT?

Mom:	MUD PIES!
Dad:	MMM! Mud pies YUMMY! We go MAKE some! (**Mom** and **Dad** start to leave.)
Mom:	If only me could remember RECIPE! (**Mom** and **Dad** exit.)

For Post-Play Pondering:

1. Do you think most kids would be happier if their parents were dumber—or smarter? Why?

2. When are your parents most likely to let you do what you want? When are they least likely?

3. What are two disadvantages of obeying parents? What are two advantages?

4. Do you think Christian parents are generally tougher on their kids than other parents are? Should they be?

5. If you ever become a parent, what will you do to keep your family from turning out like the one in the skit?

Other Scriptures for Study:

Exodus 20:12; Luke 15:11-32

Officer Bob

Topic: Alcohol and Other Drugs
Scripture for Study:
Ephesians 5:15-18

The Scene: A school gym

The Simple Setup: Set three chairs in a row at stage right, facing a podium, which is set at
stage left. **Kids 1, 2,** and **3** should wear school clothes; **Officer's** costume should suggest a
police uniform (blue shirt and slacks, dark tie, badge, and reflective sunglasses, for example).
Principal should wear a suit. Have a sheet of poster board depicting a bottle of beer, a marijuana leaf, and a variety of pills for **Officer Bob.**

Other Options: If you like, set up an easel next to the podium for the chart.

The Characters:

Officer Bob, a tough policeman who almost snarls when he talks
Principal, a dull speaker with a nasal voice
Kid 1, bored and sarcastic
Kid 2, same as 1
Kid 3, same as 1 and 2

*(As the skit begins, **Kids 1, 2,** and **3** sit in a row, facing the podium that stands at stage left.)*

Kid 1: Oh, MAN! Another BORING ASSEMBLY!

Kid 2: Did you see who the SPEAKER is? Some COP!

Kid 3: WOW, I wonder what he might SAY? Could it have something to do
with...SUBSTANCE ABUSE?

Kid 1: *(Groaning)* Ohhh...just say NO!

Kid 2: We have one of these practically every MONTH!

Kid 3: Don't you HATE it when they get up there and say the SAME STUFF
OVER AND OVER?

Kid 1: *(In a singsong voice)* Don't drink THIS! Don't smoke THAT!

Kid 2: Do they think we're even LISTENING?

Kid 3: UH-oh...here comes the PRINCIPAL!

(**Principal** *enters and stands at podium.*)

Principal: (*With a boring, nasal voice*) Good AFTERNOON, students, and welcome to today's ASSEMBLY. Our special guest is OFFICER BOB from the POLICE DEPARTMENT. His subject is ALCOHOL AND OTHER DRUGS. I KNOW you will give him your COMPLETE ATTENTION.

Kid 1: Yeah, RIGHT!

Principal: And NOW, let's give a big HUFNAGLE-HIGH WELCOME to...OFFICER BOB.

(**Kids 1, 2,** *and* **3** *roll their eyes and clap slowly and without enthusiasm as* **Principal** *exits and* **Officer Bob** *comes to podium.*)

Officer Bob: ALCOHOL and OTHER DRUGS! You think you know all ABOUT 'em, but you DON'T! And TODAY I'm going to FILL YOU IN on EXACTLY what you NEED to KNOW!

Kid 2: Oh, BROTHER.

Kid 3: WAKE me when it's OVER.

Officer Bob: Let's start with ALCOHOL. It's a GREAT place to start, and the SOONER you start DRINKING it, the BETTER!

Kid 1: HUH?

Kid 2: WHAT did he say?

Officer Bob: SOME of you kids started drinking when you were FIVE, SIX YEARS OLD. GOOD for YOU! Keep it UP! As for the REST of you, you've got a lot of CATCHING UP to do! You drink maybe a COUPLE BEERS a DAY. What's the MATTER with you? You ought to be downing a SIX PACK with every MEAL, or at least a FIFTH of WHISKEY on your way HOME from SCHOOL!

Kid 3: Am...am I DREAMING, or WHAT?

Kid 1: I can't BELIEVE this!

Officer Bob: NOW, on to OTHER drugs. You've probably heard of MARIJUANA—also known as POT, GRASS, REEFER, or MARY JANE. WHATEVER you call it, NOW'S the time to start SMOKING it! It might be HARD at first to ROLL YOUR OWN marijuana cigarettes, but with PRACTICE you can DO IT! And don't buy those little BAGGIES of pot, either. Buy it by the BRICK—you'll SAVE MONEY in the LONG run!

Kid 2: Did he say what I THINK he said?

Kid 3: This can't be HAPPENING!

Officer Bob: As for the so-called HARDER drugs, they're just a little harder to GET. But they're WORTH it! CRACK, HEROIN, UPPERS, DOWNERS, ANGEL DUST, INHALANTS—you NAME it, it's OUT there! Don't WAIT to become a USER! Take a LOOK at these CHARTS I brought. Memorize what EACH of these drugs LOOKS like. If you don't learn to RECOGNIZE them, how will you be able to BUY them?

Kid 1: 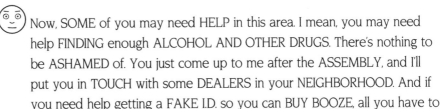 WHAT?

Officer Bob: Now, SOME of you may need HELP in this area. I mean, you may need help FINDING enough ALCOHOL AND OTHER DRUGS. There's nothing to be ASHAMED of. You just come up to me after the ASSEMBLY, and I'll put you in TOUCH with some DEALERS in your NEIGHBORHOOD. And if you need help getting a FAKE I.D. so you can BUY BOOZE, all you have to do is ASK!

Kid 2: REALLY?

Officer Bob: Well, we've got just a FEW MINUTES LEFT. Are there any QUESTIONS?

Kid 3: (Raising hand) Uh…you WANT us to use alcohol and other drugs? I mean, all the OTHER speakers tell us to stay AWAY from that stuff!

Officer Bob: YEAH, yeah. I've HEARD all those guys and their "JUST SAY NO." They sound like a BROKEN RECORD. I say, "Just say YES"!

Kid 1: (Raising hand) But…WHY do you want us to use these things? Aren't they supposed to be BAD for us?

Officer Bob: Of COURSE they're bad for you! That's the whole POINT! There's TOO MANY of you stinkin' TEENAGERS in the world! If you don't start DRINK-ING and SMOKING this stuff, how are we ever going to get RID of you?

(**Principal** enters, running to podium.)

Principal: Uh…THANK you, Officer Bob…I think it's time for you to GO…

Officer Bob: I'LL tell you what TIME it is! It's time to THIN OUT the TEENAGE POPULA-TION! You brats make my life MISERABLE with your AWFUL MUSIC and your WEIRD CLOTHES and your UGLY HAIRCUTS!

Principal: (*Pushing* **Officer Bob** *away from podium*) Uh…THANK you, Officer Bob…

(**Principal** *begins to drag* **Officer Bob** *offstage.*)

Officer Bob: (*As he is being dragged offstage*) I HATE you kids! You're a bunch of JUVENILE DELINQUENTS! And don't forget to pick up a PAMPHLET on your way out—it tells how to make LSD in your VERY OWN KITCHEN!

(**Officer Bob** *and* **Principal** *exit.*)

Kid 1: (*After a pause, standing*) WELL! Who did THAT guy think he was?

Kid 2: (*Standing*) YEAH! Telling us we HAVE to use alcohol and other drugs!

Kid 3: (*Standing*) We don't have to do ANYTHING he says!

(**Kids 1**, **2**, *and* **3** *look at each other, frowning.*)

Kid 3: Hey, WAIT a minute…

Kid 1: Now if we USE that stuff, people will think it was HIS idea!

Kid 2: I HATE these assemblies!

Kid 3: Me, TOO! Let's go have a DRINK. (*They start to leave.*)

Kid 1: Or NOT.

Kid 2: YEAH.

Kid 3: WHATEVER. (*They exit.*)

For Post-Play Pondering:

1. When it comes to drugs and alcohol, do you feel you've heard it all before? Why or why not?

2. Do you think adults warn against alcohol and other drugs (a) because they care about kids, (b) because they don't want kids to have fun, (c) because other adults expect them to, or (d) for some other reason?

3. Why do you suppose the Bible warns against drunkenness? How could this apply to using marijuana, heroin, or other drugs?

4. If it were legal for you to use alcohol and other drugs, would it be OK? Why or why not?

5. Pretend you have to come up with an anti-drug slogan to replace "Just say no." What would it be?

Other Scriptures for Study:

Proverbs 20:1; 23:29-35; 1 Peter 1:13-16

The Fight

Topic: Science and the Bible
Scripture for Study:
Romans 1:18-20

The Scene: A wrestling arena

The Simple Setup: No set is needed. Before the skit begins, "plant" **Fan 1** and **Fan 2** in the audience; these two actors should stand as needed to shout their lines. Put as much or as little effort into the wrestlers' costumes as you like. At a minimum, give **Science Boy** a lab coat or tape an atomic symbol (electrons whirling around a nucleus) on his shirt; give **Theologian** a mask and a suit. To go whole-hog, use real high school wrestling outfits with lab coat and mask added. **Referee** should wear white shirt and dark slacks.

Other Options: If you like, rope off a "ring" for the wrestlers.

The Characters:

   Science Boy, threatening but intellectual pro wrestler

   The Masked Theologian, menacing but well-educated pro wrestler

   Referee, dramatic and loud

   Fan 1, big-mouthed cheerleader for science

   Fan 2, annoying supporter of religion

*(As the skit begins, **Fans 1** and **2** are "planted" in the audience. **Referee** enters and goes to center stage.)*

Referee: LADIES...AND...GENTLEMEN! WELCOME to the FIGHT of the CENTURY! The UNIVERSAL WRESTLING FEDERATION presents a NO-HOLDS-BARRED GRUDGE MATCH to the FINISH! *(Points stage right.)* In THIS corner...weighing ONE HUNDRED AND SEVENTY-FIVE POUNDS...the MASTER OF THE MICROSCOPE...the CRUNCHER OF THE CALCULATOR...the TERRORIST OF THE TEST TUBE...IT'S...SCIENCE BOY!

*(**Science Boy** enters and stands stage right, waving at the audience.)*

Fan 1: YEA, SCIENCE BOY!

Science Boy: E equals MC SQUARED! The ELECTRON'S charge is NEGATIVE! LIGHT travels at ONE HUNDRED EIGHTY-SIX THOUSAND MILES PER SECOND!

Fan 2: BOO! Go back to your LABORATORY, Science Boy!

Referee: *(Points stage left.)* And in THIS corner...weighing TWO HUNDRED AND TWENTY-THREE POUNDS...the BOSS OF BIBLE VERSES...the

RACKETEER OF RELIGION…the STEAMROLLER OF STAINED-GLASS WINDOWS…it's…THE MASKED THEOLOGIAN!

(**Theologian** *enters and stands stage left, waving at the audience.*)

Fan 2: We LOVE you, Masked Theologian!

Theologian: Pauline EPISTLES! HIGHER CRITICISM versus LITERAL INTERPRETATION! INTERTESTAMENTAL PERIOD, FOUR HUNDRED THIRTY-TWO TO FIVE B.C.!

Fan 1: BOO! Get out of the RING, you freaky FANATIC!

(**Science Boy** *and* **Theologian** *approach* **Referee**.)

Referee: OK, boys…you know the RULES! No THEORIZING BELOW THE BELT! First man to beat the OTHER to a PULP WINS!

(**Referee** *moves to rear of stage and watches. Wrestlers face each other, snarling. Until further notice they "stalk" each other, moving in a slow circle face to face, looking as if they might pounce at any time.*)

Fan 1: C'MON, Science Boy! Use your LOGIC HOLD on that FEATHERBRAIN!

Fan 2: HEY, Masked Theologian! FRY that geek with a LIGHTNING BOLT from HEAVEN!

Science Boy: (*To his opponent*) The WORLD…is ROUND!

Theologian: I KNOW!

Science Boy: You DO?

Theologian: SURE!

Science Boy: But I thought you RELIGIOUS types believe the earth is FLAT! Isn't that what your BIBLE says?

Theologian: NO, of COURSE not! The Bible mentions the FOUR CORNERS OF THE EARTH, but that's just an EXPRESSION. People still use that expression TODAY!

Science Boy: OH. Well, NEVER MIND.

Fan 1: HEY, let's see some BLOOD! This isn't a PANEL DISCUSSION, you know!

Fan 2: YEAH! Everybody KNOWS SCIENCE and the BIBLE can't get ALONG! Let's BREAK some BONES!

Theologian: Uh...SCIENCE can't PROVE that GOD DOESN'T EXIST!

Science Boy: That's CORRECT.

Theologian: WHAT? You ADMIT that science can't ANSWER every QUESTION?

Science Boy: Of COURSE. We may be able to answer some of the "WHAT" questions, but not the "WHYS." We never said we COULD!

Theologian: OH. Well, NEVER MIND.

Fan 1: HEY! Quit AGREEING with each other!

Fan 2: YEAH! This is supposed to be the FIGHT of the CENTURY!

Science Boy: Um...SCIENCE has shown that the SIMPLEST LIFE FORMS appeared FIRST, followed by organisms of INCREASING COMPLEXITY!

Theologian: GOOD!

Science Boy: What do you mean, "GOOD"?

Theologian: That's what the BIBLE says, TOO! And the MOST complex came LAST—HUMAN BEINGS!

Science Boy: (Stops the stalking moves and scratches his chin.) You know, we may have more in COMMON than I THOUGHT.

Theologian: (Also stops and scratches his chin.) You may be RIGHT!

Fans 1 and 2: BOOOOOOO!

Fan 1: We came here to see you guys KILL each other!

Fan 2: I want my MONEY back!

Fan 1: Me, TOO!

(**Fans 1** and **2** leave.)

Theologian: I SAY, Science Boy...why don't we go get a bite to EAT, and we can discuss this FURTHER?

Science Boy: EXCELLENT idea. (*Gestures offstage.*) After YOU, Masked Theologian!

Theologian: Oh, you can call me THEO! (*They exit.*)

(**Referee** *returns to center stage.*)

Referee: Uh…SORRY, folks! I didn't think these guys could EVER get along! But be here NEXT week for ANOTHER fight of the century, when CAPTAIN FOOTBALL meets DOCTOR CHESS CLUB! GOOD NIGHT!

(**Referee** *exits.*)

For Post-Play Pondering:

1. Do you think science and the Bible are natural enemies? Why or why not?

2. Have the things you've heard at church or at home about Creation ever conflicted with what you've been taught at school? If so, what did you do about that?

3. What do you believe about how the world and its inhabitants came to be? How did you form that opinion?

4. As scientific theories change over the years, do you think they'll come to agree more with the Bible, or less? Why?

5. With which of the characters in the skit do you identify more? Why?

Other Scriptures for Study:

Job 37:14-24; Romans 12:18; Revelation 4:11

Mental Detector

Topic: Violence
Scripture for Study:
Matthew 5:21-22

The Scene: A school entryway

The Simple Setup: No set is needed. You will need the following props: a pair of binoculars for **Principal**; a small electronic device (TV remote control, calculator, or something similar) for **Vice Principal**; a backpack for **Honor Student**. **Principal** and **Vice Principal** should wear suits; **Tough Kid** should wear an outfit your group will associate with rebellion against authority; **Honor Student** should wear "good" school clothes. Choose group members to vocalize the "thoughts" of **Tough Kid**, **Honor Student**, **Principal**, and **Vice Principal**, delivering those lines at an offstage (and unseen) microphone. As an alternative, record the "thoughts" before the skit. At the appropriate time, play these recordings into the offstage mike.

Other Options: If your **Vice Principal** can manage it, have him or her act like a Peter Lorre-type mad scientist's assistant.

The Characters:
Principal Brown, a dictator
Vice Principal Green, groveling but resentful
Tough Kid, dangerous-looking
Honor Student, innocent-looking
Tough Kid's Thoughts, offstage voice
Honor Student's Thoughts, offstage voice
Principal Brown's Thoughts, offstage voice
Vice Principal Green's Thoughts, offstage voice

*(As the skit begins, **Principal** is looking through binoculars that are pointed slightly above the audience. **Vice Principal** stands nearby, rubbing hands together and looking hopefully at **Principal**.)*

Principal: Vice Principal GREEN!

Vice Principal: YES, Master! (*Pauses.*) I mean, YES, Principal BROWN!

Principal: We have a PROBLEM!

Vice Principal: What IS it, your iron fistedness?

Principal: The STUDENTS are showing up again!

Vice Principal: Oh, I'm SORRY. We send them HOME every afternoon, and they keep coming BACK!

Principal: I suppose we'll have to let them IN. YOU know...the LAW, and all that.

Vice Principal: Yes, I suppose SO.

Principal: But we're going to keep them under CONTROL! Do you HEAR me? We're not going to have...an INCIDENT!

Vice Principal: No, of COURSE not! NO INCIDENTS!

Principal: Now, did you order that EQUIPMENT?

Vice Principal: Oh, YES! It arrived this MORNING! Just THINK—we'll be the FIRST SCHOOL IN TOWN with...a MENTAL DETECTOR!

Principal: (*Lowering binoculars*) WHAT did you say?

Vice Principal: I said...we'll be the FIRST SCHOOL IN TOWN with a MENTAL DETECTOR!

Principal: MENTAL detector? I told you to order a METAL detector!

Vice Principal: METAL detector? What's THAT?

Principal: It's a device that ALERTS US to anyone who's carrying a WEAPON! What in the world did YOU order?

Vice Principal: A MENTAL detector! It detects anyone who's even THINKING of being violent!

Principal: WHAT? This machine can actually READ THOUGHTS?

Vice Principal: GUARANTEED! I got it from the HOME SHOPPING NETWORK!

Principal: (*Looking through binoculars again*) Hmm. I guess we'll have to TRY it. We can't keep those students locked out FOREVER. Let them IN—but just ONE AT A TIME!

(**Vice Principal** *exits.*)

Principal: MENTAL detector? I never HEARD of such nonsense...

(**Vice Principal** *returns.*)

Vice Principal: The doors are OPEN. Here comes the first STUDENT!

(**Tough Kid** *enters, scowling and swaggering.*)

Principal: (To **Tough Kid**) YOU, there! Go over to Vice Principal GREEN!

(**Tough Kid** *looks disgustedly at* **Principal** *and walks to* **Vice Principal**.)

Vice Principal: Uh…good MORNING…student. I just need to pass this DEVICE over your BRAIN before you can go IN.

(**Vice Principal** *takes small electronic device from pocket and holds it next to head of* **Tough Kid**, *who faces audience, folds arms across chest, and frowns.*)

Tough Kid's (*Via offstage microphone*) Man, when I get IN here, I'm gonna take the place
Thoughts: APART! I'm gonna BREAK THE WINDOWS, SPRAY-PAINT THE WALLS, and SET THE DESKS ON FIRE!

(**Tough Kid**, *surprised, looks around as if to see where the voice is coming from.*)

Principal: (To **Tough Kid**) All RIGHT, you! We don't NEED YOUR kind around here! Get out of my SCHOOL! OUT! (**Tough Kid** *gives* **Principal** *a dirty look and exits.*)

Vice Principal: It…it WORKS!

Principal: (*Looking through binoculars*) Maybe. But I could have TOLD you that kid was TROUBLE! When you've been in the education game as long as I have, you can ALWAYS tell the bad apples just by LOOKING!

Vice Principal: Of COURSE, your bad-temperedness! (*Looking offstage*) Oh, here comes ANOTHER student!

(**Honor Student** *enters, smiling and wearing backpack. Goes to* **Vice Principal**, *who holds device next to* **Honor Student's** *head.*)

Principal: Just let this one IN, Green! ANYBODY can see this is a FINE student with NO VIOLENT TENDENCIES WHATSOEVER!

Honor Student's (*Via offstage microphone*) These administrators are such LOSERS! But I
Thoughts: showed THEM! They'll NEVER GUESS I was the one who SLASHED THEIR CAR TIRES THIS MORNING!

(**Honor Student**, *angry, looks around as if to see where the voice is coming from.*)

Principal: Why, you…(To **Vice Principal**) Green, take this PSYCHO to the SECURITY GUARD in FRONT!

(**Vice Principal** *leads* **Honor Student** *offstage.*)

Principal: Let the AIR out of MY tires, will ya? I'll show YOU, you little...

(**Vice Principal** returns.)

Principal: 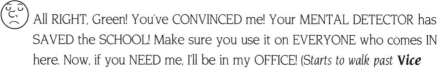 All RIGHT, Green! You've CONVINCED me! Your MENTAL DETECTOR has SAVED the SCHOOL! Make sure you use it on EVERYONE who comes IN here. Now, if you NEED me, I'll be in my OFFICE! (Starts to walk past **Vice Principal**)

Vice Principal: Uh...EXCUSE me, your grouchiness...but you can't go IN yet.

Principal: What are you TALKING about?

Vice Principal: You said to use the mental detector on EVERYONE! (Holds device next to **Principal's** head.)

Principal: Not on ME, you idiot! I'm the PRINCIPAL!

Principal's Thoughts: (Via offstage microphone) I ought to BREAK this numbskull's NECK! No, that would be too QUICK! Better to use a STEAMROLLER! Or a TRASH COMPACTOR! Or SLOW POISON...

Vice Principal: Oh, I'm SORRY, your viciousness. But you can't come IN.

Principal: What?

Vice Principal: Your THOUGHTS are MUCH too VIOLENT.

Principal: I'll show you VIOLENCE! Trying to keep me out of my own SCHOOL...

Vice Principal: NOW, now, your furiousness. Don't make me call the SECURITY GUARD.

Principal: You'll be SORRY, you PIPSQUEAK! I'll see to it that you never work in this district AGAIN! (Starts to exit.) You should try that mental detector on YOURSELF! You'll find there's nothing to DETECT! (Exits.)

(After a pause, **Vice Principal** holds device up to own head.)

Vice Principal's Thoughts: (Via offstage microphone) Ooh, that big BUFFOON! I'd like to take a SLEDGEHAMMER and—

(**Vice Principal** quickly takes device away from head and looks around, embarrassed.)

Vice Principal: OOPS! (Pauses, clears throat, looks offstage.) NEXT!

(**Vice Principal** exits.)

For Post-Play Pondering:

1. Which do you think would be more effective in curbing school violence: a metal detector or a "mental" detector? Why?

2. Can you tell from looking which people might be violent? Why or why not?

3. Is violence a problem in your school? What have school officials done about it?

4. What do you think is the best solution to the problem of violence at school? in society at large? in the world?

5. If we had a working "mental" detector right now, would you want it used on you? Why or why not?

Other Scriptures for Study:

Leviticus 19:16-18; Psalm 139:23-24; Proverbs 3:31-32; Hebrews 4:12-13

The Price Is Slight

Topic: Materialism
Scripture for Study:
Philippians 4:11-13

The Scene: A TV studio

The Simple Setup: No set is needed. For props have a hand-held microphone (or something resembling one) for **Buck** and a sign that says "Applause and Cheering" for **Cheryl**. Station the **Announcer** at an offstage microphone, where he or she can also provide the "buzzer" sound effect vocally. Dress **Paul** in a Bible-times outfit (robe, sandals, Middle Eastern head covering), with a handwritten "Paul" name tag stuck on his robe; put **Buck** in a suit and **Cheryl** in a glamorous dress. Explain to group members that they'll be cheering and applauding as cued by the sign.

Other Options: If you like, plant a few helpers in the audience to get the cheering and applause started.

The Characters:

    Paul, humble apostle
    Buck Barter, pushy game show host
    Announcer, overly excited offstage voice
    Cheryl Ferret, lovely model

*(As the skit begins, the stage is empty. **Paul** waits at the back of the room, behind the audience.)*

Announcer: 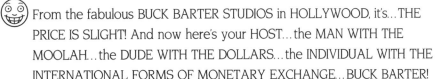 From the fabulous BUCK BARTER STUDIOS in HOLLYWOOD, it's...THE PRICE IS SLIGHT! And now here's your HOST...the MAN WITH THE MOOLAH...the DUDE WITH THE DOLLARS...the INDIVIDUAL WITH THE INTERNATIONAL FORMS OF MONETARY EXCHANGE...BUCK BARTER!

*(**Buck** enters, holding microphone and waving at audience. **Cheryl** enters, smiling, crosses the stage while holding up "Applause and Cheering" sign, and exits.)*

Buck: GREEDY GREETINGS, everyone! And welcome to THE PRICE IS SLIGHT...the show where you can win FABULOUS PRIZES by guessing how much they COST. Let's find our FIRST CONTESTANT! He's a member of our STUDIO AUDIENCE...Mr. APOSTLE PAUL! Come on DOWN!

*(**Cheryl** enters, smiling, crosses the stage while holding up "Applause and Cheering" sign, and exits. **Paul** makes his way from the back of the room, looking around as if trying to figure out what's going on. Finally he steps onto the stage.)*

Buck: 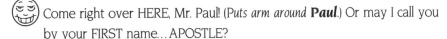 Come right over HERE, Mr. Paul! (*Puts arm around **Paul**.*) Or may I call you by your FIRST name...APOSTLE?

Paul: Uh...actually, my FIRST name is PAUL. "APOSTLE" is sort of a TITLE.

Buck: Oooh, a TITLE! SO, Paul, what's your LAST name?

Paul: Well, I guess I don't HAVE one, exactly. My WHOLE name is PAUL of TARSUS. But it used to be SAUL. See, my name CHANGED after I met the LORD on the road to—

Buck: All RIGHT, all RIGHT! ENOUGH with the NAME! Let's get on with the GAME! And you know how our game WORKS, don't you, Paul?

Paul: Er...not REALLY.

Buck: WHAT? Where have you BEEN for the last forty years?

Paul: In the ANCIENT ROMAN EMPIRE, mostly.

Buck: I take it the TV RECEPTION isn't very GOOD there. So I'll EXPLAIN the GAME. We show you FABULOUS PRIZES, YOU guess how much they COST...and, if you're RIGHT, you get to KEEP them!

Paul: Oh, THAT'S OK. YOU don't have to give me any PRIZES.

Buck: WHAT?

Paul: I don't NEED anything.

Buck: Oh, Paul, you're such a KIDDER!

Paul: But the LORD has PROVIDED ALL that I NEED.

Buck: Ah, but do you have all that you WANT? THAT'S what life is all ABOUT... getting everything your little heart DESIRES!

Paul: Well, I don't THINK so. For me to live is CHRIST, and to DIE is—

Buck: WHOA, big fella! Lighten UP! I'm sure you'll change your MIND when you see our FIRST FABULOUS PRIZE! Tell him all ABOUT it, Announcer!

Announcer: It's...a set of SOLID GOLD PATIO FURNITURE!

(**Cheryl** enters, smiling and holding up "Applause and Cheering" sign; she poses and sweeps a hand toward an invisible display.)

Announcer: From NORTH AMERICAN NONESSENTIALS comes the ULTIMATE in OUTDOOR COMFORT!

(**Cheryl** *puts sign behind her back.*)

Announcer: You'll be the ENVY of the entire THIRD WORLD as you lounge away the hours on this GLEAMING, TWENTY-FOUR-PIECE SET featuring SEATS of CORINTHIAN LEATHER! And WHILE you relax, you can watch this…GIANT-SCREEN TV!

(**Cheryl** *holds up sign, sweeps a hand toward another invisible display, then puts sign behind her back.*)

Announcer: A full FIFTY YARDS WIDE and just HALF AN INCH THICK, this state-of-the-art HOME THEATER will give you YEARS of ENJOYMENT…unless your NEIGHBORS get an even BIGGER one! From JEALOUSY ELECTRONICS!

Buck: SO, Paul…what do you say to THAT?

Paul: Is that FIRST CORINTHIANS LEATHER, or SECOND CORINTHIANS LEATHER?

Buck: HUH?

Paul: Never MIND.

Buck: Time to guess how much it COSTS, Paul. For the SOLID GOLD PATIO FURNITURE…the GIANT-SCREEN TV…the whole display next to which the lovely CHERYL FERRET is now STANDING…what is the MANUFAC-TURER'S SUGGESTED RETAIL PRICE?

Paul: Hmm. THIRTY PIECES OF SILVER?

(**Announcer** *makes buzzer sound.*)

Buck: SORRY, Paul! The ACTUAL price is TWELVE MILLION, SEVEN HUNDRED AND FORTY-NINE THOUSAND, NINE HUNDRED AND NINETY-FIVE DOLLARS AND NINETY-NINE CENTS! You get…NOTHING!

Paul: THAT'S OK.

Buck: What do you MEAN, "THAT'S OK"? You should be TEARING YOUR HAIR OUT!

Paul: I have LEARNED, in WHATEVER state I AM, to be CONTENT.

Buck: CONTENT? I HATE that word! You'll change your TUNE, Paulie, when you see our NEXT fabulous prize! TELL him, Announcer!

Announcer: From STIFFANY JEWELERS, it's the WORLD'S LARGEST KEY RING!

(**Cheryl** *holds up sign, sweeps a hand toward another invisible display, then puts sign behind her back.*)

Announcer: A full TEN FEET in diameter, PURE PLATINUM, encrusted with DIAMONDS, EMERALDS, RUBIES, and MOON ROCKS! You'll never lose your keys AGAIN! A great place to put the keys to... YOUR NEW CAR!

(**Cheryl** *holds up sign, sweeps a hand toward another invisible display, then puts sign behind her back.*)

Announcer: Yes, it's the legendary HUMZEE ARMORED PERSONNEL CARRIER! Be the FIRST on your block to own the SAME vehicle driven by MOVIE STARS and ARMY PRIVATES! Weighs over THIRTY TONS! Gets nearly TWO MILES TO THE GALLON! From HUMZEE, the car that says, "GET OUT OF MY WAY!"

Buck: Bet you can't say "no" to THAT, Mr. Apostle!

Paul: NO. I mean, YES... I CAN say "no."

Buck: You INGRATE! Don't you realize how much this stuff is WORTH?

Paul: NO... but I know how much it COSTS. See, you pay a HEAVY PRICE when you spend your life chasing after more and more THINGS.

Buck: OH, so you think you're BETTER than we are, eh?

Paul: NO, I didn't—

Cheryl: I think he's INSULTING us, Buck!

Paul: But I—

Cheryl: I say, let's STONE him!

Paul: STONE me? Oh, no... not AGAIN.

(*Shaking his head,* **Paul** *exits.* **Cheryl** *angrily runs after him.*)

Buck: SORRY, folks! We'll have to SCREEN our CONTESTANTS more CAREFUL-LY! Join us TOMORROW, when we'll tell a NORMAL person to... COME ON DOWN! (*Calling offstage*) Hey, CHERYL! Save a rock for ME! (*He exits.*)

Announcer: Promotional considerations provided by BEVERLY HILLS SAND AND GRAVEL! When you want to throw STONES, it's the way to GO! Mr. Barter's WARDROBE by FRED'S OF HOLLYWOOD! This is GRUBBY OLSON, reminding you that... no matter what those BIBLE-TIME WEIRDOS say... THE PRICE... IS SLIGHT!

For Post-Play Pondering:

1. What "fabulous prizes" would appeal to you more than the ones that were offered in the skit?

2. What kind of "price" might someone pay for chasing after more and more things? Have you ever seen this happen?

3. Should a Christian be content without a car? a CD player? a VCR? a computer? How do you decide?

4. Why do people in different parts of the world seem content with different amounts of "things"? What conclusions can you draw from that?

5. Do you think most teenagers are more materialistic, less materialistic, or just as materialistic as most adults are? Why?

Other Scriptures for Study:

Ecclesiastes 4:5-8; 1 Timothy 6:6-10; Hebrews 13:5-6

Mind Game

Topic: Making Decisions
Scripture for Study:
James 1:5-8

The Scene: A teenager's room

The Simple Setup: Place a chair center stage, facing the audience. Put a Bible on the floor next to the chair. For the "brain" tossed around by the "Harlem Lobetrotters," use one of the following: a brain-shaped foam toy, a rubber or plastic brain available in novelty shops, or a head of cauliflower. **Kid** can be casually dressed; the other actors should wear basketball uniforms or gym clothes.

Other Options: If possible, have the basketball players practice their running, tossing, and whistling before the skit.

The Characters:

> **Kid,** a teenager agonizing over a decision
> **Hummingbird Hawkins,** mischievous basketball player
> **Tornado Turner,** his hot-tempered teammate
> **Lemonhead Lewis,** their clumsy teammate

▼ ▼ ▼ ▼ ▼ ▼ ▼ ▼

*(As the skit begins, **Kid** is sitting alone, center stage, facing the audience and praying. A Bible is next to the chair.)*

Kid: So, ANYWAY, God…I've got this really TOUGH DECISION to make. Should I take this AFTER-SCHOOL JOB at the MALL? I mean, I need the MONEY to buy CLOTHES and stuff and SAVE UP for COLLEGE…but I'd probably have to miss YOUTH GROUP a lot, and I'd have less time for HOME-WORK…So you'll HELP me make this DECISION, right? Give me some WISDOM, OK? Um…AMEN. *(Looks around.)* Oh, MAN…I don't feel any WISER than I did BEFORE I prayed! I thought God was going to HELP me! I HATE making decisions! How am I supposed to—

*(Suddenly the three basketball players—**Hummingbird**, **Tornado**, and **Lemonhead**—enter. They are whistling a tune that sounds a little like "Sweet Georgia Brown." **Hummingbird** carries something that looks like a human brain. The three players run in a circle around **Kid**, continuing to whistle.)*

Kid: HEY! Who are YOU? What are you doing in my ROOM?

*(**Hummingbird**, **Tornado**, and **Lemonhead** abruptly turn and start running in the opposite direction, still circling **Kid** and whistling.)*

Kid: HEY! I said, who are YOU? And what are you doing in my ROOM?

(**Hummingbird**, **Tornado**, and **Lemonhead** *stop running and whistling.*)

Hummingbird: Who ARE we? Don't you KNOW? We're just THE MOST FAMOUS BAS-KETBALL TEAM in the HISTORY OF THE WORLD! Haven't you ever heard of...THE HARLEM LOBETROTTERS?

Kid: The Harlem LOBETROTTERS?

Hummingbird: YEAH! I'm HUMMINGBIRD HAWKINS. (*Points at* **Tornado**.) This is TORNADO TURNER.

Tornado: (*Growling*) UNNNNH.

Hummingbird: (*Pointing at* **Lemonhead**) And this is LEMONHEAD LEWIS.

Lemonhead: Um...uh...HI?

Hummingbird: RIGHT, Lemonhead! "HI!" (*To* **Kid**) The man's not exactly DR. STEPHEN HAWKING, you know what I MEAN?

Kid: But...The Harlem LOBETROTTERS? Is that LOBE, as in...

Hummingbird: BRAIN! Lobes of the BRAIN! FRONTAL lobe, BACKAL lobe, and all those OTHER lobes! SPEAKING of which...(*Holds up the object that resembles a brain.*) I got YOUR brain right HERE!

Kid: My BRAIN! (*Holds sides of head as if it hurts.*) What are you doing with my BRAIN?

Hummingbird: Why, we're...PLAYING with it!

(**Hummingbird**, **Tornado**, and **Lemonhead** *start running again, circling* **Kid** *and whistling their tune; this time they toss the "brain" back and forth to each other as they run.*)

Kid: HEY! You can't DO that!

(*Players stop whistling, but keep running and tossing.*)

Hummingbird: SURE we can! You might say we're playing a little...MIND GAME!

Kid: (*Holding sides of head*) I don't NEED this right now, OK? I'm trying to make a REALLY TOUGH DECISION!

Hummingbird: You don't SAY! Does it feel like your brain is being...TOSSED BACK AND FORTH?

(**Hummingbird**, **Tornado**, *and* **Lemonhead** *stop running, but keep throwing the "brain" to each other.*)

Kid: YES! I...I keep PRAYING about it, asking God to help me make the RIGHT CHOICE, but...I just don't KNOW! What if I make the WRONG DECISION? What if God isn't really HELPING me? What if...God isn't even LISTENING?

Hummingbird: Yeah, you got a PROBLEM, all right!

Kid: So quit throwing my BRAIN around! I NEED it!

Hummingbird: (*Tosses "brain" to* **Tornado**, *who holds onto it.*) Are you saying we have to STOP PLAYING?

Kid: YES!

Tornado: (*Growling and angrily squeezing "brain" between his hands*) GRRRRR!

Kid: OW! Quit SQUEEZING my BRAIN!

Hummingbird: NOW, NOW, Tornado. I'm sure the kid didn't REALLY mean we had to stop. (*To* **Kid**) RIGHT?

Kid: Uh...RIGHT! (*Players resume tossing.*) It's just that...I don't know WHAT to think! I keep going BACK AND FORTH...I can't MAKE UP MY MIND! I talked to the YOUTH PASTOR at CHURCH about it, but all he did was tell me to LOOK UP SOME BIBLE VERSES!

Hummingbird: Oh, YEAH? Which ONES?

Kid: Um...JAMES ONE, FIVE THROUGH EIGHT.

Hummingbird: HUH. Well, no point in looking 'em UP. I'm sure they wouldn't HELP. RIGHT, Lemonhead? (*Tosses "brain" to* **Lemonhead**, *who drops it.*)

Lemonhead: OOPS!

Kid: OUCH! That's my BRAIN, remember?

(**Lemonhead** *picks up "brain" but drops it again.*)

Lemonhead: OOPS! Brain is SLIPPERY!

(**Lemonhead** *picks up "brain" again but keeps dropping it.*)

Kid: OW! OUCH! You're KILLING me! (*Picks up Bible and starts looking up verses.*) I'll try ANYTHING—even looking up those BIBLE VERSES!

(*Lemonhead* *finally gets control of "brain" and hugs it to his chest.*)

Kid: JAMES ONE, FIVE THROUGH EIGHT...HERE it is...(*Reading*) "If any of you lacks WISDOM, he should ask GOD, who gives GENEROUSLY to ALL without finding FAULT, and it will be GIVEN to him. But when he ASKS, he must BELIEVE and not DOUBT, because he who DOUBTS is like a WAVE OF THE SEA, BLOWN and TOSSED by the WIND. THAT man should not think he will receive ANYTHING from the Lord; he is a DOUBLE-MINDED man, UNSTABLE in all he DOES." (*Pauses.*) HEY! That's IT! I've already ASKED God for WISDOM. Now I have to BELIEVE He's GIVEN it to me...make the BEST decision I CAN...and stick WITH IT!

Hummingbird: Oh, RATS! I suppose this means we have to give your BRAIN back.

Kid: Well, I would APPRECIATE it.

(*Lemonhead*, *looking sad, hands* **Kid** *the "brain."*)

Tornado: GRRRRR...

Hummingbird: Don't WORRY, guys. We'll find ANOTHER one. In FACT, I heard the kid NEXT DOOR is trying to decide whether to BREAK UP WITH HIS GIRL-FRIEND!

Lemonhead: Oh, GOODY!

Tornado: (*Grunting approval*) UNNNNH!

(**Hummingbird**, **Tornado**, *and* **Lemonhead** *exit, whistling their tune. After a pause*, **Kid** *stands with "brain" in one hand and Bible in the other.*)

Kid: HMMM. I wonder if there's a way to get THIS...(*Holds up Bible.*) into THIS! (*Holds up "brain," then tries to stick Bible into "brain" from a couple of different angles as he or she exits.*)

For Post-Play Pondering:

1. What's the toughest decision you've had to make in the last year? Did you feel like the kid in the skit? Why or why not?

2. What does it mean to be "double-minded"? How can a person become more "single-minded"?

3. Do you really believe that God is willing to give wisdom to anyone who asks? Why or why not?

4. If you had to pick two friends and two adults to help you make a tough decision, who would they be?

5. Have you ever looked in the Bible to help you make a decision? If not, why not? If so, what happened?

Other Scriptures for Study:

Psalm 143:10; Matthew 26:36-42; Romans 12:2

Rescue 912

Topic: What Jesus Did for Us

Scripture for Study:
Ephesians 2:1-10

The Scene: A TV studio

The Simple Setup: No set is needed. **William Shockner** should wear a suit; the others may wear casual clothes.

Other Options: If your stage has theatrical lighting, try darkening the platform. Train a spotlight on **Shockner** while he's speaking; when he isn't, switch the spot to the young person who's telling his or her story.

The Characters:

William Shockner, somber and dramatic host
Kayla Thomas, teenager
Troy Hannigan, teenager
Shannon Spencer, teenager

*(As the skit begins, the stage is empty. **Shockner** enters and stands center stage, facing the audience.)*

Shockner: What happens when people face CERTAIN DEATH, and only ONE PERSON can RESCUE them?

HELLO…I'm WILLIAM SHOCKNER. Every DAY, all over the WORLD, people get themselves into situations from which they CANNOT ESCAPE without HELP. That's when they turn to the One who, for THOUSANDS OF YEARS, has DEVOTED himself to RESCUE. Welcome to…RESCUE 912. *(Pauses.)* Our FIRST story takes place in a SMALL TOWN like so many OTHERS. It started out as an ORDINARY DAY for KAYLA THOMAS.

*(**Kayla** enters and stands near **Shockner**.)*

Shockner: But before the day was OUT, Kayla would face…THE ULTIMATE DANGER. It was a matter of…ETERNAL LIFE OR DEATH.

Kayla: I'd always thought it was SAFE to go the way I was GOING. I followed the RULES, more or less. But ONE DAY this SPEAKER came to our church, and he said that no matter HOW many GOOD things I did, they couldn't CAN-CEL OUT the BAD ones. And if I was going to have ETERNAL LIFE instead of ETERNAL DEATH, all the BAD STUFF had to be CANCELED OUT. I was SCARED! All of a sudden, the WRONG THINGS I'd done seemed to WEIGH

DOWN on me like a MILLION TONS. I felt as though I were going to be CRUSHED! But the speaker said JESUS had PAID for my sins and all I had to do was CALL on him and ask him to RESCUE me. I wasn't sure I could DO it; I was SWEATING, afraid people would LAUGH at me. But finally I CALLED OUT, and he was there in a FLASH. He RESCUED me. It was as if he LIFTED this CRUSHING WEIGHT so that I could be FREE. Nobody ELSE could have done it. Without HIM, I'd still be TRAPPED under all that stuff, with NO HOPE.

Shockner: After her DRAMATIC RESCUE, Kayla would NEVER be the SAME.

Kayla: Well, NO. I'm pretty much the SAME.

Shockner: I mean…you were so GRATEFUL that you did whatever you could to THANK your RESCUER.

Kayla: Um…not REALLY. I've pretty much LOST TOUCH with him. I thought of sending a THANK-YOU NOTE, but I'm kind of BUSY, you know? (*She exits.*)

Shockner: Uh…I…Well, our NEXT story comes from the MEAN STREETS of a BIG CITY.

(**Troy** *enters and stands near* **Shockner**.)

Shockner: TROY HANNIGAN was in TROUBLE…BIG trouble.

Troy: My LIFE was a MESS. I was into DRUGS. I belonged to a GANG. I DROPPED OUT of SCHOOL. Every morning I woke up WONDERING if I would LIVE to see that NIGHT. One day I couldn't TAKE it anymore. I climbed to the TOP of the HIGHEST BRIDGE in TOWN. I looked down into the RUSHING WATERS of the RIVER. I didn't REALLY want to END it all, but what CHOICE did I have? Then, all at once, I REMEMBERED something I'd heard from my MOM when I was LITTLE…that if I CALLED on JESUS, he would RESCUE me. It was hard to believe that even HE could rescue me after all I'd done. But there was nowhere else to TURN. I CALLED, and he SAVED me from JUMPING. Instead of being the END of my life, it was like a NEW BEGINNING. He helped me get off DRUGS and quit the GANG. I went back to SCHOOL. My OLD friends hardly RECOGNIZED me. If Jesus hadn't been WITH me on that BRIDGE, I wouldn't be here TODAY.

Shockner: After his DRAMATIC RESCUE, Troy told ALL HIS FRIENDS how THEY, TOO, could be rescued.

Troy: WHAT, are you KIDDING? I'd be, like, TOTALLY EMBARRASSED!

Shockner: WELL, then, you…showed how GRATEFUL you were by VOWING to SERVE your RESCUER for the REST OF YOUR LIFE.

Troy: I don't THINK so! I mean, once I turned my LIFE around, I could start being a SUCCESS! THAT'S my vow—to MAKE SOMETHING of my LIFE! (*He exits.*)

Shockner: But…I…(*Sighs.*) Our FINAL story takes place at a REMOTE SUMMER CAMP.

(**Shannon** *enters and stands near* **Shockner.**)

Shockner: SHANNON SPENCER thought she was there for FUN AND GAMES. But on the LAST NIGHT, she made a STARTLING DISCOVERY.

Shannon: We were all around the CAMPFIRE. The SPARKS were flying HIGH into the SKY. I'd ALREADY called out to Jesus to RESCUE me way back when I was LITTLE—and he'd DONE it. But I'd never realized how HARD it had been for him to save me. Our COUNSELOR told us that as soon as Jesus arrived on his RESCUE MISSION, practically everybody REJECTED him. He was ARRESTED, even though he hadn't done anything WRONG. They SPIT on him and took his CLOTHES. They jammed a sharp CROWN OF THORNS on his head. They NAILED him to a CROSS. He had to HANG there, BLEEDING, while they made FUN of him. Finally He DIED. He had to DIE to rescue me!

Shockner: After learning the DETAILS of her DRAMATIC RESCUE, Shannon was OVERWHELMED with SADNESS AND GRATITUDE.

Shannon: HUH?

Shockner: When you found out that your RESCUER had died a PAINFUL DEATH to SAVE you, you'd never take your rescue for GRANTED again.

Shannon: OH. Sure. Whatever.

Shockner: WHATEVER?

Shannon: YEAH. I mean, let's not get all EMOTIONAL. It happened over 2000 years ago, after all. (*She exits.*)

Shockner: (*After a pause*) I…uh…well…there you HAVE it. THREE dramatic RESCUES. Three people who, when all hope was LOST, were SAVED at the cost of an INNOCENT MAN'S LIFE. Three SECOND CHANCES. Three people who…when you get right DOWN to it…COULDN'T CARE LESS.

For RESCUE 912, I'm WILLIAM SHOCKNER. GOOD NIGHT. (*He starts to leave, talking to himself*) 😑 Is...is it ME? Did I MISS something? (*Shaking his head, he exits.*)

▶For Post-Play Pondering:

1. How do people usually act when they've narrowly escaped death? Why do you suppose the kids in this skit didn't act that way?

2. What did the host expect from the kids? Was it fair of him to expect those things?

3. If you barely survived a fiery plane crash, do you think it would change your life in any way? If so, how? If not, why not?

4. Why do some Christians talk about being "saved"? Do you think this word is a good one to describe what happens when you become a Christian? If not, what word would you use?

5. If you've been "rescued" by Jesus, what did he rescue you from? How have you responded to him in return?

Other Scriptures for Study:

Mark 15:16-37; John 3:16-17; 2 Corinthians 8:9

Vengeance Is Mine

Topic: Loving Your Enemies
Scripture for Study:
Romans 12:17-21

The Scene: A car

The Simple Setup: Place two chairs next to each other, center stage, facing the audience. Dress **Mr. Gutwrench** in white shirt, tie, and slacks; **Amanda** may dress casually. Have an offstage helper play recorded sound effects (for the squealing brakes and crash) or improvise them vocally at an offstage microphone.

Other Options: If you wish, make **Mr. Gutwrench** look older by powdering his hair with cornstarch and giving him a few facial wrinkles with an eyeliner pencil.

The Characters:

    Amanda, nervous driver education student
    Mr. Gutwrench, driver ed teacher and major lunatic

*(As the skit begins, the actors sit next to each other, center stage, facing the audience. **Amanda** sits in the stage-left chair, **Mr. Gutwrench** in the stage-right chair.)*

Mr. Gutwrench: ALL right, Amanda. Just turn the KEY in the IGNITION, and let's get STARTED.

*(**Amanda** reaches in front of her, as if she's sitting in the driver's seat of a car, and turns an imaginary key. Then she places her hands on the invisible "steering wheel.")*

Amanda: THERE. Did I do it RIGHT, Mr. GUTWRENCH?

Mr. Gutwrench: Just FINE…although you MIGHT want to CLOSE THE DOOR before you start DRIVING.

Amanda: *(Closing imaginary door)* OOPS! SORRY! I guess I'm a little NERVOUS, this being my first DRIVER EDUCATION CLASS and all.

Mr. Gutwrench: No need to be NERVOUS, Amanda. Today we'll just concentrate on the MOST BASIC PART of driving—the ONE thing EVERY new driver needs to learn FIRST.

Amanda: Uh…STEERING?

Mr. Gutwrench: NO.

Amanda: GAS PEDAL?

Mr. Gutwrench: NO.

Amanda: BRAKE? TURN SIGNAL? PARALLEL PARKING?

Mr. Gutwrench: No, no, and no. Those are all ICING ON THE CAKE, Amanda. I'm talking about the most FUNDAMENTAL skill every driver MUST have. (*Pauses.*) GETTING REVENGE!

Amanda: Wh—WHAT?

Mr. Gutwrench: Getting REVENGE, Amanda! VENGEANCE! GETTING BACK at OTHER drivers who DARE to DO YOU WRONG!

Amanda: But…aren't there OTHER things I need to work on FIRST? I heard the OTHER driver ed teacher, Mr. CLUTCHWELL, always starts with LEARNING TO OPEN THE GLOVE COMPARTMENT!

Mr. Gutwrench: Ah, YES…Mr. CLUTCHWELL. The one who STOLE MY CHAIR that time in the FACULTY LOUNGE. The one who SPILLED COFFEE ON MY PANTS at the PTA MEETING! The one who FAILED TO REWIND MY INSTRUCTIONAL VIDEO of HIDEOUS CAR ACCIDENTS! THAT Mr. Clutchwell! I WILL DESTROY HIM! (*He pauses to get control of himself.*) AHEM. Perhaps Mr. Clutchwell does not REALIZE that GETTING REVENGE is the MOST IMPORTANT PART OF DRIVING.

Amanda: But I thought the most important part was…DRIVING DEFENSIVELY.

Mr. Gutwrench: NO! You must drive ANTISEPTICALLY! You must CLEANSE THE ROAD of the OFFENSIVE VERMIN! Vengeance is MINE, do you hear? Vengeance is MINE!

Amanda: Uh…isn't there a BIBLE VERSE that says vengeance belongs only to GOD?

Mr. Gutwrench: BIBLE verse? Amanda, let's not mix CHURCH and STATE! Now, put the transmission in DRIVE and pull into TRAFFIC.

Amanda: (*Pantomiming shifting gears and starting to drive*) OK…I'll TRY…

Mr. Gutwrench: You're doing FINE. Now, just ease into the… HEY! Did you SEE that? Who does that guy think he IS, pulling in FRONT of you? We must teach him a LESSON, Amanda!

Amanda:	A...LESSON?
Mr. Gutwrench:	YES! RAM HIS BUMPER! FORCE HIM OFF THE ROAD!
Amanda:	BUT...but I can't...
Mr. Gutwrench:	WE'LL show HIM! Hit the GAS and give him something to THINK about!
Amanda:	But isn't that against the LAW?
Mr. Gutwrench:	HURRY! He's getting AWAY! (*Pauses.*) AARRGH! You let him ESCAPE! Now how will we get REVENGE?
Amanda:	C-could we practice something ELSE? Maybe TURNING THE CAR RADIO ON AND OFF?
Mr. Gutwrench:	Where's your FIGHTING SPIRIT, Amanda? FORGET the RULES! PUNISH the FOOLS! (*He looks up, as if into the rear view mirror.*) WHOA! That TRUCK is TAILGATING us! I HATE tailgaters!
Amanda:	Maybe if I SPEED UP a bit...
Mr. Gutwrench:	NO! That's just what he WANTS! Show him WHAT FOR, Amanda! Hit the BRAKES! THAT'LL teach him!
Amanda:	But if I hit the BRAKES...
Mr. Gutwrench:	(*Grabbing the invisible steering wheel and stamping his foot where the brake would be*) I said, HIT THE BRAKES! Vengeance is MINE! Ha-HA! YES!

(**Offstage helper** *makes sounds of squealing brakes and crash.* **Amanda** *and* **Gutwrench** *bounce as if from the impact of a car being hit from behind.*)

Amanda:	OH! OW!
Mr. Gutwrench:	OOF!
Amanda:	(*After a pause, looking where rear view mirror would be*) Oh, NO! The whole BACK END of the CAR is SMASHED! And so is the FRONT of the TRUCK!
Mr. Gutwrench:	Ha-HA! No PROBLEM! The truck was BEHIND us, so it's HIS fault! Ah, REVENGE is SWEET!
Amanda:	(*Looking in "mirror"*) The TRUCK DRIVER is getting out...He's coming this WAY...

Mr. Gutwrench: (*Looking in "mirror"*) He's…he's…so TALL…

Amanda: At least SIX-FOOT-SIX!

Mr. Gutwrench: Probably TWO HUNDRED AND SEVENTY-FIVE POUNDS…

Amanda: And he doesn't look HAPPY.

Mr. Gutwrench: Is…is that a BASEBALL BAT in his hand?

Amanda: He looks like he wants…REVENGE!

Mr. Gutwrench: Uh…that's ALL for TODAY, Amanda! (*Pantomimes opening car door.*) There's just ONE MORE THING we need to PRACTICE…

Amanda: What's THAT?

Mr. Gutwrench: LEAVING THE SCENE OF AN ACCIDENT! (*He exits running.*)

(**Amanda** *pantomimes wearily opening car door, getting out, and closing door.*)

Amanda: I wonder if there's any ROOM left in MR. CLUTCHWELL'S CLASS. (*She exits.*)

▶ For Post-Play Pondering:

1. Does getting revenge usually feel good? Does it usually feel as good a month later? Why or why not?

2. If the government gave you a million dollars and asked you to solve the problem of "road rage," what would you do?

3. Why do you suppose God reserves vengeance to himself?

4. Which of the following "enemies" would it be hardest for you to love: (a) someone who stole your bike; (b) a terrorist who blew up a bus load of children in Israel; (c) a racist who burned down your church; (d) someone who planted drugs in your locker to get you in trouble? Why?

5. What's one movie or TV show you've seen that made revenge look like a good idea? What story idea can you create that encourages people to leave revenge up to God?

Other Scriptures for Study:
Leviticus 19:18; Proverbs 24:17-20; 1 Peter 2:19-24

Closed Encounters

Topic: The Bible
Scripture for Study:
1 Corinthians 1:18-25

The Scene: A desert mesa

The Simple Setup: No set is needed. **Kids 1, 2,** and **3** could wear any casual clothes; if you want to help identify them, however, try the following suggestions. **Kid 1:** depending on gender, "Valley Girl" outfit (upscale "mall" clothes) or "surfer dude" wardrobe (tropical print shirt and shorts, sunglasses). **Kid 2:** overalls. **Kid 3:** rapper outfit. Give Alien an all-white or metallic costume.

Other Options: For added effect, flash colored lights from offstage when the spacecraft lands and takes off. If you're really ambitious, give **Alien** a touch of extraterrestrial makeup (pointed ears, off-white skin, etc.)

The Characters:

    Alien, a dignified, otherworldly being
    Kid 1, a Valley girl or surfer dude
    Kid 2, a rural Southerner
    Kid 3, a streetwise city-dweller

▼ ▼ ▼ ▼ ▼ ▼ ▼ ▼

*(As the skit begins, the stage is empty. After a few seconds, **Kid 1** enters, crawling.)*

Kid 1: Like, I can't believe I finally MADE it! Who'd have thought CLIMBING up a CLIFF in the DESERT would be, like, HARD? I'm, like, TOTALLY SWEATY!

*(**Kid 1** lies down to rest. **Kid 2** enters from another direction, also crawling.)*

Kid 2: WHOA! FRY MY FINS and CALL ME A CATFISH! I feel like DEATH eatin' a CRACKER! They don't have hills like THIS where I come from!

*(**Kid 2** lies down to rest. **Kid 3** enters from another direction, also crawling.)*

Kid 3: MAN! Who put this ROCK TOWER in the middle of NOWHERE? They oughta have an ESCALATOR up here! *(Looks around, sees others.)* HEY! What are YOU doin'? I thought this was MY territory!

Kid 1: *(Groaning and sitting up)* OHH...I'm, like, TOTALLY WIPED!

Kid 2: *(Also sitting up)* Well, COUNT MY FLEAS and CALL ME A HOUND DAWG! What are y'all DOIN' on top of this MOUNTAIN?

Kid 1: It's, like, NOT a MOUNTAIN! It's a MESA! That means "TUBULAR" in SPANISH!

Kid 3: No WAY, airhead! It means TABLE!

Kid 1: Well, like, WHATEVER.

Kid 2: SO…what brings you folks UP here?

Kid 1: I'm, like, in the DARK! All I know is…every time we have MASHED POTATOES for dinner, some STRANGE POWER forces me to MOLD them into the shape of a MESA just like THIS one!

Kid 2: Well, TAN MY HIDE and CALL ME A WALLET! I been doin' the SAME THING, only with GRITS!

Kid 3: That's SISSY stuff! I been makin' mesas out of stuff I find in the STREET…like CIGARETTE BUTTS and STRAY BULLETS!

Kid 1: So…the THREE of us have been, like, MYSTERIOUSLY DRAWN from ALL OVER THE COUNTRY to MEET at this spot!

Kid 2: What do y'all think we're HERE for?

Kid 3: Hey, LOOK! Up in the SKY! It's a FLYING HUBCAP!

Kid 1: That is totally NOT a hubcap! It's, like…a UFO!

Kid 2: Well, DYE ME GREEN and CALL ME A MARTIAN! Looks like it's gonna land right here on this ol' ROCK!

Kid 1: Like, STAND BACK!

(They watch one of the exits as if the UFO is landing there.)

Kid 3: Look at all those LIGHTS! They're doin' a HIP-HOP kinda thing!

Kid 1: Oh, like, the DOOR is opening! This is SO COOL!

Kid 2: Well, ENERGIZE MY GASES and CALL ME A NEBULA! Here comes…a real, live ALIEN!

*(**Alien** enters.)*

Alien: GREETINGS, Earth dwellers. I am PLATTU, from the planet NEXOR in the galaxy MORGLEDEK.

Kid 1: Far OUT!

Alien: Yes, VERY far out. We on the planet Nexor have been OBSERVING you for many YEARS. I have been SENT to SHARE with you the WISDOM that could SAVE your TROUBLED WORLD.

Kid 1: Oh, COOL! It's, like, the SECRETS OF LIFE from an ADVANCED CIVILIZATION!

Kid 2: HOT DAWG! We're all EARS!

Kid 3: YEAH! Lay some WISDOM on us, man!

Alien: Very WELL. To BEGIN…you must not KILL one another.

Kid 1: Oh, that is, like, SO WISE! We must STOP THE MADNESS!

(All **Kids** nod.)

Alien: SECOND, you must tell only the TRUTH about each other.

Kid 2: You got THAT right, stranger! Truthful IS as truthful DOES!

Alien: THIRD, you must not TAKE what does not BELONG to you.

Kid 3: Right ON! That's the way to PEACE and BROTHERHOOD, you DIG?

Alien: FOURTH, you must have NO OTHER GODS before the ONE, TRUE GOD.

Kid 1: Like, WHAT?

Kid 2: Come AGAIN?

Kid 3: What's this GOD RAP, man?

Alien: I will REPEAT: You must have NO OTHER GODS before the ONE, TRUE GOD.

Kid 1: WAIT a minute! I've, like, HEARD THAT SOMEWHERE BEFORE!

Kid 3: It's from…the TEN COMMANDMENTS, man!

Kid 2: The TEN COMMANDMENTS? Well, I'll be HORNSWOGGLED! That's from…the BIBLE!

Alien: The BIBLE! YES! In MONITORING your planet, we discovered this GREAT BOOK OF WISDOM, UNMATCHED throughout the KNOWN UNIVERSE!

Kid 3: The BIBLE? Are you NUTS, man?

Kid 1: That is, like, so totally NOT COOL!

Kid 3: NOBODY believes THAT stuff anymore!

Kid 1: Like, REALLY! You're supposed to give us COSMIC wisdom! Like, WE HAVE UNLIMITED POWER WITHIN US! And EVERYTHING IS ONE! And WHEN THE MOON IS IN THE SEVENTH HOUSE and JUPITER ALIGNS WITH MARS...

Kid 2: You'd best be skedaddlin' back to your OWN planet, SPACE YANKEE! We don't need YOUR KIND around these parts!

Kid 3: That's RIGHT! Go back to your OWN 'hood...WHATEVER you are!

Kid 1: You are, like, SO UNWELCOME!

Alien: Very WELL. I will return to Nexor. It is clear that your species is not...READY...for these teachings.

(**Alien** exits.)

Kid 3: (Calling after **Alien**) NEXT time, monitor some REAL wisdom, man!

Kid 1: (Looking up as if at rising spacecraft) Like...TV GUIDE!

Kid 3: (Also looking up) Or some GANGSTA RAP!

Kid 2: (Also looking up) Or a COUNTRY MUSIC STATION!

Kid 1: (After a pause) The BIBLE! That is, like, so LAME!

Kid 3: Man, what a WASTE of TIME! Now we've got to climb DOWN from here and walk ALL THE WAY HOME!

(**Kids 1, 2,** and **3** start to exit.)

Kid 1: BUMMER! (Pauses.) NEXT time I have MASHED POTATOES, I'm, like, just going to EAT them!

Kids 2 and 3: Me, TOO!

(They exit.)

For Post-Play Pondering:

1. If creatures from other planets exist, do you think they're wiser than we are? Why or why not?

2. Do you think more people believe in the existence of extraterrestrial beings or the truthfulness of the Bible? Why?

3. What are some "wise" sayings that people like to hear these days? What are some they don't like to hear?

4. If you were on a debate team, would you use the Bible to back up any of your points? Why or why not?

5. What percentage of your own values do you suppose are based on the Bible? What are the rest based on? Why?

Other Scriptures for Study:

Psalm 12:6; Ecclesiastes 3:14-15; Matthew 24:35

Team Spirit

Topic: The Church
Scripture for Study:
John 17:20-23

The Scene: A locker room

The Simple Setup: You'll need a bench or three chairs center stage, facing the audience. **Mitch Stroppelmeyer** and **Players 1** and **2** should dress casually; **Coach** should wear sweats and a cap, and carry a notebook.

Other Options: If you like, add these props: a football for **Players 1** and **2** to toss back and forth; a whistle for **Coach** to wear around his neck; a towel to set on the bench or next to the chairs.

The Characters:

Coach, gruff but inspiring leader of the school football team
Mitch Stroppelmeyer, unmotivated player
Player 1, enthusiastic team member
Player 2, another enthusiastic team member

*(As the skit begins, **Stroppelmeyer** and **Players 1** and **2** are sitting on a bench or three chairs, facing the audience. **Coach** is in front of them, pacing back and forth.)*

Coach: SO, men...when it comes to FOOTBALL, our team is SECOND TO NONE! As you step onto that BUS, I want you to remember that when we get to Mid-Valley High, it won't MATTER that we're the VISITORS! We're going to WIN, because we have...TEAMWORK! Now, EVERYBODY on the BUS! Think VICTORY!

Players 1 and 2: *(Chanting as they get up and exit)* VICTORY! VICTORY! VICTORY!

Coach: *(After a pause)* STROPPELMEYER! Why aren't you getting on the BUS?

Stroppelmeyer: Well...I just don't feel like going to the GAME today, coach.

Coach: DON'T FEEL LIKE GOING? What, are you SICK?

Stroppelmeyer: NO, no. I just don't feel like GOING. You go on AHEAD. I'll be FINE.

Coach: Is that RIGHT? Well, exactly what are you planning to DO?

Stroppelmeyer: Oh...I thought I'd have a leisurely BRUNCH...then turn on the TV and watch a FOOTBALL game.

Coach: WATCH a football game? You're supposed to PLAY one!

Stroppelmeyer: But the games on TV are MUCH more interesting. The players are PROS! And you don't have to get all MUDDY.

Coach: MUDDY? You can't play football without getting a little DIRT on your uniform!

Stroppelmeyer: EXACTLY! That's why I MUCH prefer to watch it on TV.

Coach: Stroppelmeyer, we have a GAME to play! Now, get on the BUS and let's go to the STADIUM!

Stroppelmeyer: Oh, but the stadium is so CROWDED. And you have to find a PARKING PLACE. And the MUSIC is so OLD! All the band plays is MARCHES! And they're always out to get your MONEY—asking you to pay for HOT DOGS, SOFT DRINKS, POTATO CHIPS...

Coach: I SEE. And I suppose you don't care for the CHEERLEADERS, either!

Stroppelmeyer: Now that you MENTION it, they can be pretty OBNOXIOUS...standing up there in FRONT, waving their ARMS and trying to get everybody HYPED...even if you're not in the MOOD.

Coach: Well, if THAT'S the worst you can come up with—

Stroppelmeyer: Oh, NO, THAT'S not the WORST. The WORST is the HALFTIME SHOW. BOR-ing!

Coach: FORGET the halftime show! You're supposed to be in the GAME! Now, get your HELMET and—

Stroppelmeyer: Oh, that REMINDS me. About those HELMETS...why do we have to put THOSE on? They're UNCOMFORTABLE! It shouldn't MATTER what we wear to a game! I should be able to wear ANYTHING I WANT!

Coach: Is that SO?

Stroppelmeyer: And ANOTHER thing. We do the SAME THING EVERY TIME! Always trying to get the BALL to the GOAL POSTS! Tackle THIS, tackle THAT...FIRST down, SECOND down, THIRD down—always in the same ORDER! How about a little VARIETY?

Coach: We HAVE variety! Every PLAY is DIFFERENT!

Stroppelmeyer: Nobody asks ME what the plays should be! We always have to go by that BOOK you carry around!

Coach: LISTEN to me, Stroppelmeyer! You are a member of a TEAM! The team works TOGETHER! The team NEEDS you!

Stroppelmeyer: Oh, they don't need ME. It's not like I'm the QUARTERBACK!

Coach: A team isn't just QUARTERBACKS! We need CENTERS, FULLBACKS, RUNNING BACKS, TIGHT ENDS…

Stroppelmeyer: Those OTHER positions don't COUNT. The QUARTERBACK gets all the GLORY.

Coach: (*Looking at his watch*) We're running out of TIME, Stroppelmeyer! Are you going to be part of this team or NOT?

Stroppelmeyer: NO, I don't THINK so. You don't really need a TEAM for FOOTBALL, you know.

Coach: WHAT?

Stroppelmeyer: I can have a PERFECTLY VALID FOOTBALL EXPERIENCE all by MYSELF. It doesn't have to be on a FIELD. It can be on a GOLF COURSE, A BASEBALL DIAMOND, UNDER WATER!

Coach: How can you play football by YOURSELF?

Stroppelmeyer: Well, you don't actually have to PLAY it. You can just THINK about it. Contemplate what a FINE SPORT it is. Maybe even drink some GATORADE.

Coach: OK, Stroppelmeyer. You've convinced ME. You stay HERE and have a NICE FOOTBALL EXPERIENCE ALL BY YOURSELF. The REST of us have a GAME to play! (**Coach** *exits.*)

Stroppelmeyer: (*After a pause*) Hmph! I KNEW he didn't REALLY care whether I showed up. That's the OTHER thing I hate about football stadiums…they're full of HYPOCRITES! (*He exits.*)

For Post-Play Pondering:

1. What reasons did Stroppelmeyer give for not wanting to go to the game? Which of these are like the reasons some kids give for not wanting to go to church?

2. When you apply them to church, which of Stroppelmeyer's complaints make the most sense to you? Which make the least sense?

3. If church is like a football game, who are the players? Are the people in the pews supposed to be the spectators? If not, who is?

4. Why do most people tend to get more excited about sports than they do about being involved in the church? Do you think this is a problem? Why or why not?

5. Which of the following do you think our group needs most: (a) better "cheerleaders", (b) more "practice" time together, (c) closer teamwork, or (d) a clearer understanding of the "fundamentals" of the game? Why?

Other Scriptures for Study:

Ecclesiastes 4:9-12; Acts 2:42-47; 1 Corinthians 12:12-27

That New-Time Religion

Topic: Other Religions

Scripture for Study:
Joshua 24:14-27

The Scene: A street corner

The Simple Setup: No set is needed. Both characters may wear casual clothes (but **Kid's** shouldn't be too colorful). Give **Kid** a large backpack that contains a small notebook and at least eight objects that could pass for "idols" (toy action figures, wooden carvings, ceramic figurines, and so on).

Other Options: If you have time, find "idol" props that reflect the "gods" they're supposed to represent (a Chia Pet for the god of trees and a trophy for the god of bowling, for example).

The Characters:
> **Kid,** tired but stubborn
> **Friend,** puzzled but patient

(As the skit begins, the stage is empty. After a few moments, **Kid** enters wearily—loaded down by the weight of a large backpack. **Kid** stops center stage, panting. Next, **Kid** does what appear to be exercises: lifting hands in the air, then standing with hands folded, then kneeling, then lying face down on the floor. These "exercises" are repeated once or twice, with **Kid** getting more and more tired, until **Friend** enters.)

Friend:		HEY, there! I didn't know you were into AEROBICS!
Kid:		(Still "exercising" breathlessly) I'm…NOT…These aren't EXERCISES…I'm PRAYING…
Friend:		PRAYING? How come you're MOVING AROUND so much?
Kid:		Because SOME people pray like (lifting hands) THIS…SOME pray like (standing with hands folded) THIS…SOME pray like (kneeling) THIS…And SOME pray like (lying face down on floor) THIS. (Gets up, panting.)
Friend:		So why don't you just PICK ONE POSITION and STICK WITH IT?
Kid:		I can't do THAT! If I just go like THIS (lifting hands), the people who do THIS (standing with hands folded) might be OFFENDED. If I just go like THIS (kneeling), the people who do THIS (lying face down on floor) might be offended. (Gets up, panting.) It would be like saying ONE RELIGION is BETTER than another!
Friend:		Well, I don't—

Kid: (Looking at watch) OOPS! Time for WORSHIP! Give me a hand with this BACKPACK, will you?

(**Kid** and **Friend** struggle together, finally taking off backpack.)

Friend: WOW! This thing weighs a TON! What's IN here, anyway?

Kid: (Unzipping backpack) My OBJECTS of WORSHIP. Here's (taking out idols one at a time and placing them on the floor) the GOD OF THUNDER...the god of the HARVEST...the god of the SUN...the god of the MOON...

Friend: BOY, that's a lot of—

Kid: The god of the TREES...the god of WATER...the god of those SMELLY WEEDS with all the STICKERS on them...the god of BOWLING...

Friend: The god of BOWLING?

Kid: I didn't want to leave anybody OUT.

Friend: How can you haul all these idols AROUND? How can you even keep TRACK of them?

Kid: I HAVE to! I can't play FAVORITES, you know! That would be like saying ONE religion is RIGHT and the REST are WRONG!

Friend: But I don't—

Kid: UH-oh.

Friend: What's the MATTER?

Kid: I forgot that today is a RELIGIOUS HOLIDAY!

Friend: It IS? Which ONE?

Kid: (Takes a small notebook from backpack and flips through it.) Uh...SAINT CARBUNCLE'S DAY. Also...FESTIVAL OF THE GOLDEN WATERMELON.

Friend: GOLDEN WATERMELON?

Kid: (Returning notebook to backpack) YEAH. For SAINT CARBUNCLE'S DAY, I have to GIVE UP SAUSAGE. And for the FESTIVAL OF THE GOLDEN WATERMELON, I'm supposed to RUN AROUND THE CITY TWELVE TIMES with a GOAT ON MY HEAD. You don't happen to have a GOAT, do you?

Friend: Uh...NO.

Kid: Oh, MAN! Now people who belong to the WAY OF THE MAGIC SOYBEAN will think I don't RESPECT their BELIEFS!

Friend: I...guess you must celebrate a LOT of RELIGIOUS HOLIDAYS, huh?

Kid: NO, no. Just SEVEN HUNDRED or so. And ONE DAY A YEAR I don't celebrate ANYTHING—to show ATHEISTS that I respect THEM, too.

Friend: So...what DO you believe about God?

Kid: Uh...ME? Uh...HE...or She...is ONE. Or SEVERAL. Or MANY. And has THIRTY-SIX ARMS...or NO arms...and is INVISIBLE...or looks like a COW...or a LIGHT...He or she lives in HEAVEN...or in our HEARTS...or EVERYWHERE...or NOWHERE.

Friend: Does that make SENSE to you?

Kid: (*Returning "idols" to backpack*) It doesn't HAVE to make sense! It's RELIGION! One's as good as ANOTHER!

Friend: Actually, I thought there was only ONE way to heaven...

Kid: WHAT? Are you INSANE? How could there be only ONE way? (*Starts hitting* **Friend** *with backpack.*) You...you BIGOT! You're so INTOLERANT! Don't you know that the only RIGHT way to think is that there's NO right way to think?

Friend: Hey, CUT IT OUT! Calm DOWN! (**Kid** *stops hitting.*) LOOK, we can talk about this LATER. Let's just go have a GOOD TIME, OK? Maybe see a MOVIE?

Kid: Movie? No, that's against one of my RELIGIONS.

Friend: Uh...go have a CHEESEBURGER?

Kid: Can't do THAT, either.

Friend: Um...how about—

Kid: NOPE.

Friend: You sure have a LONG LIST of THINGS YOU CAN'T DO, huh?

Kid:	Oh, not SO long. I just can't PLAY THE GUITAR, WEAR COLORFUL CLOTHING, SEE A DOCTOR, KILL BUGS, SAY THE PLEDGE OF ALLEGIANCE, DRIVE A CAR, SERVE IN THE MILITARY, EAT PEPPERONI, GET MARRIED...or ALLOW INFIDELS TO LIVE...
Friend:	INFIDELS?
Kid:	YOU know...people who don't agree with my RELIGION. ONE of my religions, anyway.
Friend:	Oh. I...uh...just REMEMBERED. I have to be GOING. So, don't be a SNIPER! I mean, a STRANGER! Uh...see you AROUND! (*Exits, running.*)
Kid:	(*Putting on backpack*) What a WEIRDO! (*Looking around, starting to leave*) Now, where am I going to find that GOAT? (*Exits.*)

For Post-Play Pondering:

1. When you see how many religions there are in the world, how does it make you feel? If you have friends of different faiths, how do you feel about that?

2. Which of the following words apply to the decision to choose Christianity instead of other beliefs: (a) narrow-minded, (b) wise, (c) ignorant, (d) bigoted, (e) unimportant? Why?

3. In your opinion, what's the biggest difference between Christianity and other faiths?

4. If a person of another faith asked you to visit his or her place of worship, would you go? Why or why not? If you went, what would you hope to learn?

5. What are three ways in which our group could show respect for people of other faiths—without giving up our own?

Other Scriptures for Study:

Exodus 20:1-6; John 14:6

The Audition

Topic: Swearing
Scripture for Study:
Matthew 12:34-37

The Scene: A school auditorium

The Simple Setup: Place two chairs center stage, facing the audience. Both characters will need scripts as props—but since they'll probably be holding their scripts for this skit anyway, those should suffice. Actors may wear casual clothing.

Other Options: If you want to further identify the setting, you could hang a "Drama Tryouts Today" sign in the background.

The Characters:
> **Kid 1,** nervous would-be actor
> **Kid 2,** even more nervous would-be actor

▼ ▼ ▼ ▼ ▼ ▼ ▼ ▼

*(As the skit begins, **Kids 1** and **2** sit in chairs center stage, facing the audience. They hold scripts.)*

Kid 1: OOH! I'm so NERVOUS!

Kid 2: Me, TOO! I never TRIED OUT for a SCHOOL PLAY before!

Kid 1: Do you think I'll get IN? I just HAVE to get in!

Kid 2: If I DON'T get in, I'll DIE! I'll actually DIE!

Kid 1: Let's PRACTICE. I'll be the LAWYER, and you be JUROR NUMBER NINE. *(They look at scripts.)* Take it from the TOP of page THREE.

Kid 2: *(Reading, as if trying to sound adult)* "Stop trying to INFLUENCE me, you WRETCH! I can't be BOUGHT!"

Kid 1: *(Reading, as if trying to sound adult)* "Is that a FACT? Well, listen to ME, you—" *(Pauses.)* UH-oh.

Kid 2: What's WRONG?

Kid 1: Look at THIS! My character is supposed to SWEAR!

Kid 2: WOW, you're RIGHT!

Kid 1: Maybe it's just in that ONE SPOT. Let's try SCENE THREE, top of PAGE EIGHT.

Kid 2: OK. (*Reading, as if trying to sound adult*) "You have no EVIDENCE, counselor. As a matter of FACT, you're the biggest—" (*Pauses.*) OOPS.

Kid 1: (*Looks closely at script.*) OOH, that's a BAD one!

Kid 2: (*Flipping through script*) Are there MORE?

Kid 1: (*Flipping through script*) THERE'S one. And ANOTHER. And ANOTHER. (*Flipping faster*) And ANOTHER, and ANOTHER, and ANOTHER, and ANOTHER...

Kid 2: What kind of play IS this?

Kid 1: One with lots of SWEARING, I guess.

Kid 2: Oh, MAN! What are we going to DO?

Kid 1: I just HAVE to be in this play! I just HAVE to!

Kid 2: If I'm NOT in this play, I'll DIE! I'll definitely DIE!

Kid 1: OK. We have to figure something OUT.

Kid 2: RIGHT.

(**Kid 1** and **Kid 2** *sit for a few moments, racking their brains, scratching their heads.*)

Kid 1: I've GOT it! We have to find a way to keep our PARENTS from coming to the SHOW!

Kid 2: HUH?

Kid 1: We wouldn't want them to HEAR us saying stuff like THIS. But if they're not HERE, we can say anything we WANT!

Kid 2: YEAH!

Kid 1: So we just won't TELL them about the play! They won't even know we're IN it!

Kid 2: PERFECT! OK, let's PRACTICE some more.

Kid 1: No, WAIT. We'll have to remember not to tell any of our OTHER relatives, either.

Kid 2: RIGHT.

Kid 1:   Or our NEIGHBORS. THEY'D want to come.

Kid 2:   YEAH.

Kid 1:   Or the YOUTH LEADERS from CHURCH.

Kid 2:   Oh, DOUBLE yeah!

Kid 1:   OK, let's PRACTICE. Top of page THREE.

(**Kid 2** *opens mouth to read, but stops.*)

Kid 2:   HOLD it. What about our FRIENDS?

Kid 1:   What ABOUT them?

Kid 2:   We can't let our FRIENDS come to the play. They might tell our PARENTS about the SWEARING!

Kid 1:   OOH, that's RIGHT!

Kid 2:   But they won't stay away just because we TELL them to.

Kid 1:   YEAH. We'll have to PAY 'em.

Kid 2:   PAY 'em? We've got TOO MANY FRIENDS! That would cost a FORTUNE!

Kid 1:   HEY, do you want to be in this play or NOT?

Kid 2:   I HAVE to be in this play! If I'm not in this play, I'll absolutely DIE!

Kid 1:   OK, then. We'll just pay whatever it COSTS.

Kid 2:   (*Sighing*) RIGHT.   Now, let's PRACTICE. (*Reading as if trying to sound adult*) "Stop trying to INFLUENCE me, you—"

Kid 1:   Um…WAIT a minute.

Kid 2:   What NOW?

Kid 1:   There's ONE MORE PERSON we have to keep from coming to the show.

Kid 2:   WHO?

Kid 1:   GOD. YOU know how God feels about this kind of language.

Kid 2:   But how can we keep GOD away? He'll KNOW we're in it. And we can't

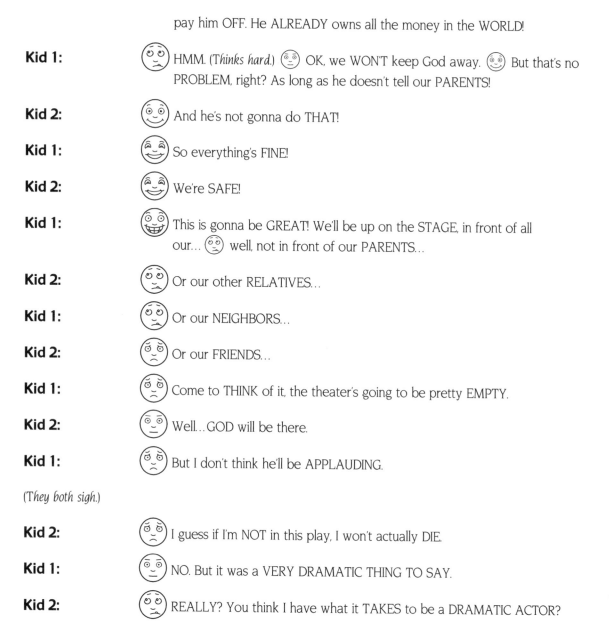

pay him OFF. He ALREADY owns all the money in the WORLD!

Kid 1: HMM. (*Thinks hard.*) OK, we WON'T keep God away. But that's no PROBLEM, right? As long as he doesn't tell our PARENTS!

Kid 2: And he's not gonna do THAT!

Kid 1: So everything's FINE!

Kid 2: We're SAFE!

Kid 1: This is gonna be GREAT! We'll be up on the STAGE, in front of all our... well, not in front of our PARENTS...

Kid 2: Or our other RELATIVES...

Kid 1: Or our NEIGHBORS...

Kid 2: Or our FRIENDS...

Kid 1: Come to THINK of it, the theater's going to be pretty EMPTY.

Kid 2: Well...GOD will be there.

Kid 1: But I don't think he'll be APPLAUDING.

(*They both sigh.*)

Kid 2: I guess if I'm NOT in this play, I won't actually DIE.

Kid 1: NO. But it was a VERY DRAMATIC THING TO SAY.

Kid 2: REALLY? You think I have what it TAKES to be a DRAMATIC ACTOR?

Kid 1: MAYBE. But stay away from COMEDIES. Especially SKITS with TWO CHARACTERS who sit on CHAIRS in the middle of the STAGE and go ON and ON about how they want to be in a PLAY.

(*They stand and start to leave.*)

Kid 2: OK.

(**Kid 1** *and* **Kid 2** *pause and look out over the heads of audience members.*)

Kid 2: Say...do you ever get the feeling you're being...WATCHED?

(**Kid 1** *and* **Kid 2** *exit.*)

►For Post-Play Pondering:

1. What would you do if you were in these characters' shoes? Why?

2. One of the characters says, "You know how God feels about this kind of language." How does God feel about it? How do you know?

3. Which do you think is worse: using God's name in vain, or using vulgar words that refer to body functions? Why?

4. Are some words OK to use around your friends but not around your parents? to listen to on television, in movies, or on CDs but not to say yourself? Why or why not?

5. If God is "watching" your language all the time, should it affect what you say? Why or why not?

Other Scriptures for Study:

Exodus 20:7; Psalms 17:3; 19:14; Ephesians 5:4-7

The Devil and Danny Webster

Topic: Spiritual Warfare

Scripture for Study:
Ephesians 6:10-18

The Scene: A park bench

The Simple Setup: Place one chair center stage, facing the audience. For props, have a music magazine for **Danny** and a sheet of paper and a pen for **Devil**. **Danny** should wear casual clothes; **Devil** could wear a suit. Note: If you'd like a girl to play the teenager's role, simply change the name to **Dani**.

Other Options: If you want to make **Devil** look more "devilish," add touches of makeup, a hairstyle, and costuming that suggest the slick and sinister (for example, pencil-thin mustache, slicked-back hair, fancy suit).

The Characters:
  Danny Webster, teenager
  Devil, well-known tempter

▼   ▼   ▼   ▼   ▼   ▼   ▼   ▼

*(As the skit begins, **Danny** sits on a chair center stage, facing the audience, looking at a music magazine.)*

Danny: *(To self)* Man, these BANDS are so COOL. I wish I could do this stuff—cut a CD, go on the ROAD, get a RECORDING CONTRACT…Next thing you know, I'd be on MTV…I'd be FAMOUS…RICH…able to do anything I WANTED. *(Sighs.)* I'd do ANYTHING to be a FAMOUS ROCK STAR…

*(Enter **Devil**.)*

Devil: Did you say…ANYTHING?

Danny: *(Looking up from magazine)* HUH?

Devil: You'd do ANYTHING to be a famous ROCK STAR, eh, Danny?

Danny: How…how did you know my NAME?

Devil: Oh, I know LOTS of things, Danny. I know the CAPITAL of SWEDEN. I know how much TWO TIMES FOUR is. I even know…the COLOR of the SHIRT you're wearing!

Danny: Well, THAT'S not much of a mystery. Who ARE you, anyway?

Devil: You can call me anything you LIKE. Some call me MR. SINISTER. Some call me SCRATCH. Some call me the CLOVEN-HOOFED ONE.

Danny: Does anybody call you…WALDO?

Devil: Uh…no, I don't THINK so.

Danny: Too BAD. You look like a WALDO to ME.

Devil: ANYWAY, some call me an ANGEL OF LIGHT. Some call me…the PRINCE OF DARKNESS.

Danny: Oh, I get it! You're…the DEVIL!

Devil: Such a BRIGHT kid. I'm beginning to LIKE you, Danny. I think we can do BUSINESS together.

Danny: BUSINESS? What KIND of business?

Devil: You WANT something, Danny. You want it BAD. And I can GIVE it to you.

Danny: You can give me a WINDY'S TRIPLE-BACON CHEESEBURGER with a MEDIUM FROSTYBITE?

Devil: Uh…NO. I'm talking about the ROCK STAR thing!

Danny: OH. You mean, you can make me a FAMOUS ROCK STAR?

Devil: Let's just say that when it comes to PULLING STRINGS, I'm a regular…STRING-PULLER.

Danny: So you can get me a CONTRACT with a BIG RECORDING COMPANY?

Devil: Well, NO. But I can show you that place at the MALL where they record you singing along with a TAPE of the TITANIC theme for TWENTY BUCKS.

Danny: What good is THAT?

Devil: Hey, it's how ELVIS got started. Sort of.

Danny: Can you get me on MTV?

Devil: I can do better than THAT. FIFTEEN MINUTES all to YOURSELF, PUBLIC ACCESS CABLE, CHANNEL NINETY-SEVEN, THREE O'CLOCK IN THE MORNING next TUESDAY!

Danny: That's not exactly what I had in MIND. What about a WORLD TOUR?

Devil: World TOUR? The TRAVEL, the HOTEL ROOMS, the NOISE of all those SCREAMING FANS...who NEEDS it? I can get you booked at the ONE-HOUR PHOTO BOOTH on TWELFTH AND WILLOW!

Danny: I don't THINK so. But once I have a CD, can you make it go PLATINUM?

Devil: Hey, who wants a PLATINUM CD? They won't even PLAY! You want good old PLASTIC, Danny.

Danny: Well...can you at least get me a GRAMMY AWARD?

Devil: No, but I can get you a nice CERTIFICATE from those LITTLE OLD LADIES at the SENIOR CENTER. Call it the GRANNY award.

Danny: Uh...no OFFENSE, but—

Devil: I KNEW you'd see it my way! (*Takes paper and pen from pocket.*) All you have to do is SIGN ON THE DOTTED LINE.

Danny: SIGN? What FOR?

Devil: It's a BUSINESS TRANSACTION, Danny. I give YOU what you want...and you give ME what I want.

Danny: And what do YOU want?

Devil: Your SOUL, Danny! I want you to sell your SOUL!

Danny: Nah, I don't THINK so.

Devil: WHAT? After all the TANTALIZING THINGS I've offered you?

Danny: Yeah, RIGHT. You couldn't even get me a CHEESEBURGER unless I PAID for it!

Devil: Well, I...I can MAKE you sign! Beware my MIGHTY POWER! (*Wiggles fingers at* **Danny.**) BOOGA-BOOGA!

Danny: Uh-HUH. You BAD.

Devil: You dare to MOCK me? Don't you realize who I AM?

Danny: Yeah. You're the guy who decided to PICK A FIGHT with the ALL-POWERFUL SUPREME BEING who CREATED THE ENTIRE UNIVERSE. Now THERE was a brilliant move.

Devil: So I made a slight MISCALCULATION! EVERYBODY makes MISTAKES!

Danny: And YOU made one coming HERE. My soul's already SPOKEN FOR anyway.

Devil: But wouldn't you rather be on MY side?

Danny: Are you KIDDING? I've read the BOOK! I know how it turns OUT! You're a LOSER—the biggest loser of all TIME!

Devil: (*Sniffling*) You...you don't have to get so PERSONAL!

Danny: Give UP. SCRAM. Get LOST.

Devil: You're RESISTING me?

Danny: You got THAT right. (*Goes back to reading magazine.*)

Devil: Oh, I HATE it when they do that! (*Starts to leave.*)

Danny: (*To self, after turning page of magazine*) HEY! Who SCRIBBLED in my MAGAZINE with a CRAYON? I bet it was my LITTLE SISTER. I'll teach HER to mess with MY things! (*Stands.*) I know...I'll pull all the STUFFING out of her TICKLE ME ELBOW DOLL! And if she tells Mom and Dad, I'll say the DOG did it! Sure, it's MEAN and DISHONEST...but she's got it COMING! (*Starts to leave; bumps into* **Devil**.) Are YOU still here? I thought I told you to get LOST! (**Danny** *exits.*)

Devil: (*After a pause*) AHHHH. That's more LIKE it. And it didn't cost me a THING! Now, THAT'S what I call...a BARGAIN! (*Exits.*)

►For Post-Play Pondering:

1. Do you think most movies, TV shows, and books make the devil look more powerful than, less powerful than, or just as powerful as he really is?

2. Is the devil stronger than you are? Why or why not?

3. If you belong to Christ, is it ever correct to say that the devil "made" you do something?

4. Is your soul "spoken" for? If so, who owns it?

5. Next time you feel tempted to do the wrong thing, what's the first thing you should do?

Other Scriptures for Study:

Romans 16:19-20; 1 Corinthians 10:13; James 1:13-15; Revelation 20:7-10

Fatal Attraction

Topic: The Resurrection
Scripture for Study:
1 Corinthians 15:12-22

The Scene: The tombs outside Jerusalem, about 33 A.D.

The Simple Setup: No set is needed. Dress both actors in Bible-era garb (robes and sandals).
Make sure **Kid 1** knows how to pronounce "Arimathea" (AHR-ih-muh-THEE-uh).

Other Options: If you have time, you could help to identify the setting by drawing a few
"tombs" on large sheets of cardboard and placing them in the background.

The Characters:

> **Kid 1**, a gung-ho teenage entrepreneur
> **Kid 2**, reluctant friend of **Kid 1**

*(As the skit begins, the stage is empty. After a few moments, **Kid 1** enters.)*

Kid 1: *(Calling offstage)* Come ON! THIS way!

*(**Kid 2** enters, looking around doubtfully.)*

Kid 2: I don't KNOW…maybe this isn't such a good IDEA.

Kid 1: What's the PROBLEM?

Kid 2: This place CREEPS me OUT.

Kid 1: WHY? It's just a bunch of…TOMBS!

Kid 2: EXACTLY! It's a bunch of TOMBS! For your information, that's where they
put DEAD PEOPLE!

Kid 1: I KNOW! So it's not like they're going to BOTHER us! They're DEAD!

Kid 2: *(Shivering)* I just hope you know what you're DOING.

Kid 1: Of COURSE I do! Have I ever NOT known?

Kid 2: Well…there was that time you wanted to make money selling CARD-
BOARD down at the TEMPLE by calling it UNLEAVENED BREAD…

Kid 1: HEY, how was I supposed to know those PHARISEES don't have a sense
of HUMOR?

Kid 2: And there was that time you tried to go into business RECYCLING SHIELDS AND HELMETS...

Kid 1: Well, if those ROMAN SOLDIERS hadn't been so ATTACHED to their ARMOR, it would have worked PERFECTLY!

Kid 2: Then there was the time...

Kid 1: ENOUGH! I get the POINT! The IMPORTANT thing is that, THIS time, my idea is FOOLPROOF!

Kid 2: But what if—

Kid 1: No IFS! This plan can't FAIL! As of THIS MOMENT, you and I are in the TOURIST ATTRACTION BUSINESS!

Kid 2: But don't we have to find the RIGHT TOMB first?

Kid 1: I already DID. It's THAT one. (*Points offstage.*) SEE? It says, 'JOSEPH OF ARIMATHEA' over the entrance. He's the guy who OWNS it.

Kid 2: I don't KNOW. This place is kind of OFF THE BEATEN PATH. They say a business needs THREE THINGS to succeed: LOCATION, LOCATION, LOCATION!

Kid 1: Don't you GET it? This place could be at the NORTH POLE, and we'd STILL draw crowds! Don't you remember how many FOLLOWERS this JESUS guy HAD?

Kid 2: Well...there WERE a lot of people CHEERING when he rode into town on that DONKEY the other day...

Kid 1: RIGHT! So everybody'll want to visit His FINAL RESTING PLACE! It's like a SHRINE! They'll bring FLOWERS!

Kid 2: Well...MAYBE...

Kid 1: We'll put up a SIGN: "SEE THE BODY!" We'll charge 'em a few SHEKELS to go INSIDE and take a PEEK. We'll sell SOUVENIRS! T-shirts that say, 'I Saw the Body...Did YOU?" And REFRESHMENTS! I can see a CONCESSION STAND right over THERE. Some FIGS, some GRAPE JUICE, some SHEEP ON A STICK...

Kid 2: But what about this JOSEPH guy? I mean, he OWNS the tomb. What if he doesn't GO for it?

Kid 1: He WILL, don't worry. We'll give him a PERCENTAGE, a little off the TOP. It'll cheer him UP. He's probably DEPRESSED, what with his FAVORITE TEACHER CRUCIFIED and all.

Kid 2: Yeah, I guess you're RIGHT.

Kid 1: OK! I'll just take a look INSIDE, see if we need to REARRANGE anything before we OPEN. (*Starts to exit in direction of "tomb."*) This is gonna be GREAT! (*Exits. There is a pause. Then* **Kid 1** *screams.*) AAUUGGHH!

(**Kid 2** *jumps, frightened. After another pause,* **Kid 1** *returns.*)

Kid 1: It's…it's…EMPTY!

Kid 2: WHAT?

Kid 1: EMPTY!

Kid 2: Let ME look. (*Exits. There is a pause. Then* **Kid 2** *screams.*) AAUUGGHH! (*After another pause,* **Kid 2** *returns.*) It's EMPTY!

Kid 1: That JOSEPH guy must have TAKEN the BODY. He'll probably build a THEME PARK around it! He just wants all the PROFIT for HIMSELF!

Kid 2: What are we gonna DO?

Kid 1: Uh…we could put up a sign that says… "SEE the…TOMB…with…NOTHING IN IT."

Kid 2: Who would pay to see THAT?

Kid 1: NOBODY.

Kid 2: I think we can FORGET this idea.

Kid 1: But it was a GREAT idea!

Kid 2: YEAH.

(*They start to exit.*)

Kid 1: Now we'll have to think of ANOTHER way to make money.

Kid 2: We could…SELL SOAP to PONTIUS PILATE. I hear he WASHES HIS HANDS a lot.

Kid 1: NAH.

Kid 2: We could...GET JOBS.

Kid 1: (*Shivering*) Ooh, STOP it! Now you're creeping ME out!

(*They exit.*)

For Post-Play Pondering:

1. Do you think that, in Jesus' day, more people were happy about the empty tomb or upset about it? Why?

2. What kinds of "problems" does Jesus' empty tomb cause for people today?

3. How might your life be different if Jesus hadn't risen from the dead?

4. Which of the following is hardest for you to believe: (a) that Jesus was born of a virgin, (b) that he is God's Son, (c) that he healed people, (d) that he died on a cross, or (e) that he rose from the dead? Why?

5. In your own words, how would you explain to the characters in the skit what happened to Jesus' body?

Other Scriptures for Study:

John 20:1-18; Acts 13:26-37; 1 Peter 1:1-5

The Garden

Topic: Caring for God's Creation
Scripture for Study:
Genesis 1

The Scene: The outdoors, long ago

The Simple Setup: For **Serpent**, you'll need a snake puppet (or sock puppet made to look like a snake). Station the puppeteer center stage, behind a piece of scenery, such as a large sheet of cardboard fastened to a small table and painted to look like a bush. Place two chairs at the sides of the scenery, slightly forward, facing the audience. (Note: If you have a puppet stage, use it instead of the scenery.) If possible, clothes for **Edna** and **Steve** should look primitive (fake fur or torn cloth, for example). For props use two rakes, hoes, or other gardening tools.

Other Options: To set the scene before the actors enter, you might want to play six to ten seconds of recorded jungle noises from a sound effects CD or tape.

The Characters:

    Serpent, a crafty snake
    Edna, teen granddaughter of Adam and Eve
    Steve, Edna's brother

*(As the skit begins, the performing area appears empty except for two chairs, center stage, facing the audience and flanking a piece of scenery. The **Serpent** and its puppeteer are already hiding behind the scenery. After a few moments **Edna** and **Steve** drag themselves in, each carrying a rake, hoe, or other gardening tool.)*

Edna:	*(Sitting down)* Ohhhh…I HATE TILLING.
Steve:	*(Sitting down)* And I hate TOILING.
Edna:	TILLING and TOILING…that's all we ever DO. We're just KIDS! We should be hanging out at the MALL!
Steve:	The MALL? MALLS won't be invented for THOUSANDS of YEARS! This is, like, the DAWN of HISTORY!
Edna:	Yeah, I KNOW. It wasn't too long ago that ADAM and EVE were invented.
Steve:	Yep. GRANDPA ADAM and GRANDMA EVE. *(Pauses)* This is all THEIR fault, you know.
Edna:	WHAT is?

Steve: All this TILLING and TOILING! It's that stupid CURSE!

Edna: If only they hadn't listened to that SERPENT. If only they hadn't eaten the FORBIDDEN FRUIT from that TREE. Then they wouldn't have gotten THROWN OUT of the GARDEN OF EDEN!

Steve: And WE wouldn't be spending all our time fighting THORNS and ROCKS, growing FOOD by the SWEAT of our BROW!

Edna: TOILING and TILLING.

Steve: TILLING and TOILING.

Edna: It's not EASY being Adam and Eve's GRANDCHILDREN.

Steve: I KNOW, Edna.

Edna: That's RIGHT, Steve.

(Suddenly **Serpent** pops up from behind scenery.)

Serpent: SSSSSSO! EDNA and STEVE, is it? Reminds me of OLD TIMES!

Edna: LOOK! It's a TALKING SNAKE!

Serpent: PLEASE! I'm a SERPENT! "SNAKE" sounds so ORDINARY!

Steve: A TALKING SERPENT…Where have I heard THAT before?

Edna: Are YOU…

Serpent: YES, that's ME. I knew your GRANDPARENTS. LOVELY couple. A bit GULLIBLE, perhaps, but LOVELY.

Steve: Well, you can CRAWL BACK under your ROCK, serpent. We're not INTERESTED in FORBIDDEN FRUIT.

Serpent: Oh, I wouldn't DREAM of trying THAT scam again. I'm here to HELP.

Edna: Help with WHAT?

Serpent: With that awful CURSE! With all that TOILING and TILLING!

Steve: You're going to help us with our CHORES? Nothing PERSONAL, pal, but I think you'd have a HARD TIME holding a RAKE.

Serpent: Oh, I can do better than THAT. I can FIX it so you won't have to TILL or TOIL ever AGAIN!

Edna: REALLY?

Steve: CAREFUL, Sis! It's a TRICK!

Serpent: No TRICK! Just COMMON SENSE. For EXAMPLE, aren't you TIRED of PRUNING all these TREES and BUSHES?

Edna: THAT'S for sure!

Serpent: Well, WHO NEEDS TREES AND BUSHES? Just CUT 'EM ALL DOWN!

Edna: But isn't it GOOD to have trees and bushes?

Serpent: Ah, but it's BETTER to MAKE things out of them! IMPORTANT things like...TOOTHPICKS! And SAWDUST! And what you don't USE, you can BURN UP in a big FOREST FIRE! SLASH and BURN! Yes, I like the SOUND of THAT!

Steve: But I thought GOD said we should be STEWARDS of the earth...YOU know, use it WISELY.

Serpent: What could be wiser than CLEARING THE LAND to make room for FUN THINGS—MOVIE THEATERS and SHOPPING MALLS, for example? Are you a SHADE FREAK or something? Are you ADDICTED to OXYGEN?

Edna: So we get RID of the PLANTS. What NEXT?

Serpent: The ANIMALS, of course. Isn't that a PAIN, taking care of those DUMB THINGS? They're a bunch of...BEASTS!

Steve: But Grandpa ADAM and Grandma EVE thought the animals were SPECIAL. They even gave the animals NAMES!

Serpent: As I SAID, your grandparents weren't exactly ROCKET SCIENTISTS. You need to make your life EASIER! REDUCE the animal population! Make some of 'em EXTINCT! The REST you can put in little CAGES! POKE 'em with STICKS! SHOW 'em who's BOSS!

Edna: Even SERPENTS?

Serpent: Present company EXCEPTED.

Steve: Let me see if I've got this STRAIGHT. We CUT DOWN THE PLANTS and BEAT UP THE ANIMALS. Anything ELSE?

Serpent: GARBAGE!

Edna: EXCUSE me?

Serpent: GARBAGE! You spend so much time PICKING UP GARBAGE around this place! Think how much SIMPLER life would be if you just LEFT IT ON THE GROUND!

Steve: But wouldn't the earth become one big TRASH HEAP?

Serpent: Hey, YOU don't have to worry about THAT! Let your KIDS and GRAND-KIDS figure it out!

Edna: Isn't that kind of…SELFISH?

Serpent: SHELLFISH! That REMINDS me! You can get rid of those pesky SEA ANIMALS by dumping a little TOXIC WASTE in the water!

Steve: TOXIC WASTE? What's THAT?

Serpent: Oh, I FORGOT. That comes LATER…along with POLLUTION and PESTICIDES. About the time they invent MALLS, I believe.

Edna: So YOU want us to make our lives EASIER by DESTROYING the world God CREATED for us to LIVE in.

Serpent: I couldn't have said it better MYSELF.

(**Edna** and **Steve** stare at each other for a moment before speaking.)

Edna and Steve: (Speaking together) OK!

Serpent: BELIEVE me, you won't REGRET thisssssss!

(**Edna** and **Steve** get up and start to leave.)

Steve: PARDON us, but we've got things to DO!

Edna: PLACES to BURN, CREATURES to SQUEEZE!

Steve: No more TILLING!

Edna: No more TOILING!

(**Edna** and **Steve** exit.)

Serpent:  (After a pause) What a NICE pair of KIDS. Lucky for ME, it looks like...BRAINS don't run in the FAMILY!

(**Serpent** exits behind scenery.)

▶For Post-Play Pondering:

1. Do you think God really cares what we do with the world he created? Why or why not?

2. Is it wrong to cut down a tree? To use pesticides? To keep an animal in a cage? How do you decide?

3. If Adam and Eve could take a look at your neighborhood, what do you suppose they'd think? Would they see it as an improvement on the Garden of Eden?

4. How do you feel about the condition in which previous generations have left the environment? What do you wish they'd done differently? What are you glad they did?

5. Fifty years from now, how do you think people will describe your generation's attitude toward God's creation? How do you hope they'll describe it?

Other Scriptures for Study:

Psalm 24:1-2; Revelation 11:16-18

He's Coming Soon

Topic: Christ's Return

Scripture for Study:
1 Thessalonians 4:16–5:11

The Scene: LeeAnne's room

The Simple Setup: Put a row of four chairs (to represent a bed) center stage, facing the audience. **LeeAnne** should have her hair in rollers or a tinting cap and her face smeared with a green or white "mask"; she should wear a dumpy robe or long nightshirt and jeans plus slippers. **Guy** should wear dirty clothes—or other garb that would suggest to your group that he isn't ideal dating material. **Cindy** can wear casual clothes. For props provide a couple of books or magazines. Ask a helper to provide the doorbell or knocking sound offstage; decide beforehand on which side of the stage the imaginary door will be located.

Other Options: To further identify the setting, you might use a real bed and hang a few posters in the background.

The Characters:

LeeAnne, a self-absorbed girl
Cindy, her no-nonsense friend
Guy, a slob

▼ ▼ ▼ ▼ ▼ ▼ ▼ ▼

*(As the skit begins, **Cindy** sits, reading, on the "bed" center stage.)*

Cindy: *(Calling offstage)* LEEANNE? When is that GUY coming to GET you?

LeeAnne: *(From offstage)* I don't KNOW exactly! But it'll be SOON!

Cindy: Then shouldn't you be getting READY?

LeeAnne: I AM getting ready! *(Enter **LeeAnne**, made up and dressed as noted in "The Simple Setup.")*

Cindy: Well, shouldn't you be getting ready a little FASTER? I mean, this guy could show up any TIME, right?

LeeAnne: Yeah. But don't WORRY. I'll be READY. *(She sits next to **Cindy** and starts reading, too.)*

Cindy: So, TELL me about this guy.

LeeAnne: Oh, he's WONDERFUL! He's COMPASSIONATE and LOVING, and he really CARES about me.

Cindy: WOW! How did you MEET him?

LeeAnne: We met a LONG TIME ago. My PARENTS introduced me to him. I was just a LITTLE KID back then, but the OLDER I get, the more SURE I am that we're MEANT to be TOGETHER.

Cindy: This sounds SERIOUS!

LeeAnne: Oh, it IS! I could NEVER feel this way about ANYONE ELSE. Even when we're APART, it's like he's always WITH me…in my HEART.

Cindy: He sounds pretty SPECIAL, all right. (*Pauses.*) So…shouldn't you be getting READY?

LeeAnne: I WILL, I WILL. (*Yawns.*) Right after I take a NAP. (*Lies down.*)

Cindy: A NAP? THIS is no time for a NAP! This GREAT GUY is coming to GET you, and you look like some kind of KILLER CLOWN!

LeeAnne: I do NOT! I look FINE!

Cindy: YEAH, for a HORROR MOVIE! How can this guy take you ANYWHERE looking like THAT? Or is he taking you to a CARNIVAL FREAK SHOW?

LeeAnne: Of COURSE not! He's taking me to a VERY ELEGANT PLACE. It's a MANSION. A BEAUTIFUL HOME he's been building JUST FOR ME.

Cindy: Well, unless you're planning to live in the FURNACE ROOM, you'll be OUT OF PLACE in such a FANCY HOUSE, WON'T you? So get READY, girl!

LeeAnne: Aw, it's too HARD to get ready. I'll just stay like THIS.

Cindy: Like THAT? He'll take one LOOK at you and RUN in the other DIRECTION!

LeeAnne: Oh, NO, he won't. He HAS to take me with him. He PROMISED, and he ALWAYS keeps his promises.

Cindy: YEAH? Well, what have you done for HIM?

LeeAnne: Um…

Cindy: (*After a pause*) I'm WAITING.

LeeAnne: I'm THINKING! (*Pauses.*) OK. I've ALWAYS ACCEPTED EVERY GIFT he's given me.

Cindy: Well, THAT'S mighty GENEROUS of you. That must have been QUITE a SACRIFICE.

LeeAnne: (*Looking at her fingernails*) YEAH. It was the LEAST I could do.

Cindy: I'm SURE. (*Pauses.*) Y'know, I'm starting to WONDER what this guy SEES in you.

LeeAnne: (*Stands and poses as if she were a model.*) Must be my NATURAL BEAUTY and FASHION SENSE.

Cindy: RIGHT.

(**Offstage helper** *makes doorbell or knocking sound.*)

Cindy: That must be HIM! Come ON! Get READY!

LeeAnne: Why BOTHER?

(**Cindy** *goes to imaginary door and opens it.* **Guy** *enters, slouching and dressed as noted in "The Simple Setup."*)

Guy: YO! (*Wipes his nose on his sleeve, snorting loudly.*) Is LEEANNE here? (*Clears his throat and pretends to spit on the floor.*)

Cindy: (*To* **LeeAnne**) Is...is THIS the guy you've been talking about?

LeeAnne: Well, NO...but... he's kind of CUTE, isn't he?

Cindy: WHAT?

LeeAnne: I'm TIRED of WAITING for that OTHER guy. I'll go with THIS one.

Cindy: WHAT?!?

LeeAnne: (*To* **Guy**) HI, big boy!

Guy: HEY, babe! Let's FLY! (*He burps loudly.*)

(**LeeAnne** *starts to leave with* **Guy**, *then pauses.*)

LeeAnne: (*To* **Cindy**) Oh...if that OTHER guy shows up, just tell him...he shouldn't have TAKEN so long!

(**LeeAnne** *and* **Guy** *exit.* **Cindy** *closes the "door."*)

Cindy: 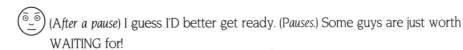 (*After a pause*) I guess I'D better get ready. (*Pauses.*) Some guys are just worth WAITING for!

(*She exits.*)

For Post-Play Pondering:

1. In what ways did the description of "the guy" fit Jesus? In what ways was LeeAnne like a person waiting for Jesus to return?

2. What does it mean to "get ready" for Jesus to come back?

3. Do you feel ready for Jesus to return? Why or why not?

4. How would you describe LeeAnne's relationship with the guy for whom she was waiting? How is that relationship like your relationship with Jesus? How is it different?

5. If Jesus came back today, what two things would you most wish you'd done last week? What two things would you be most glad you'd done?

Other Scriptures for Study:

Matthew 25:1-13; 2 Peter 3:3-14

The Kid Who Loved Porcupines

Topic: Lifestyle Choices
Scripture for Study:
Jeremiah 2:17-19

The Scene: A doctor's office

The Simple Setup: You'll need a long, sturdy table center stage to represent an examination table. **Doctor** (who can be played by either gender) should carry a clipboard with one or more papers on it. **Larry** should wear casual clothes, including a jacket—which covers an old, light-colored sweatshirt which you've dotted with dozens of dime-sized spots of red paint or food coloring. If possible, have **Doctor** wear a white lab coat, a stethoscope, or both.

Other Options: To further identify the setting, add such details as white paper or a sheet covering the table, a stack of magazines on the table, a framed certificate, or a human heart poster on the wall.

The Characters:
>   **Larry**, a tough-guy teenager
>   **Doctor**, friendly but firm

(As the skit begins, **Larry** sits on a table at center stage. He wears a jacket. He looks around, swinging his legs back and forth.)

Larry: Man, what's KEEPIN' that DOCTOR? I've read these stupid ol' magazines TWICE! Whadda they THINK, that I got all DAY? They think that just because I'm a KID, my time isn't worth—

(**Doctor** enters with clipboard.)

Doctor: SO, you must be LARRY. I'm Dr. KLINE.

Larry: HEY, it's about TIME, Doc! I had to read so many of these READER'S DIGESTS, I'm ready to condense somebody's FACE. You know what I MEAN? (Punches left hand with right fist.)

Doctor: I'm…uh…SORRY you had to WAIT so long. It's been a busy MORNING. We had two patients with—

Larry: YEAH, yeah, whatever. Let's just hope you're not like that LAST doctor I saw.

Doctor: 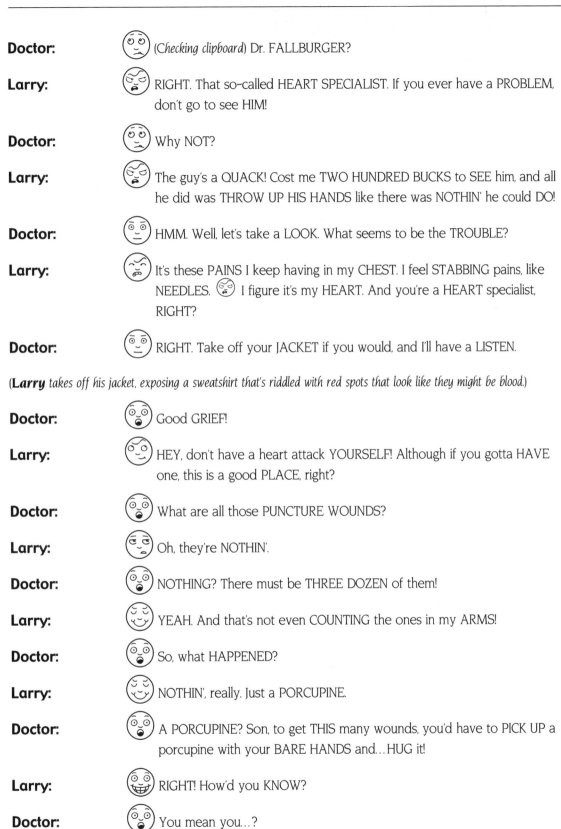 (*Checking clipboard*) Dr. FALLBURGER?

Larry: RIGHT. That so-called HEART SPECIALIST. If you ever have a PROBLEM, don't go to see HIM!

Doctor: Why NOT?

Larry: The guy's a QUACK! Cost me TWO HUNDRED BUCKS to SEE him, and all he did was THROW UP HIS HANDS like there was NOTHIN' he could DO!

Doctor: HMM. Well, let's take a LOOK. What seems to be the TROUBLE?

Larry: It's these PAINS I keep having in my CHEST. I feel STABBING pains, like NEEDLES. I figure it's my HEART. And you're a HEART specialist, RIGHT?

Doctor: RIGHT. Take off your JACKET if you would, and I'll have a LISTEN.

(**Larry** *takes off his jacket, exposing a sweatshirt that's riddled with red spots that look like they might be blood.*)

Doctor: Good GRIEF!

Larry: HEY, don't have a heart attack YOURSELF! Although if you gotta HAVE one, this is a good PLACE, right?

Doctor: What are all those PUNCTURE WOUNDS?

Larry: Oh, they're NOTHIN'.

Doctor: NOTHING? There must be THREE DOZEN of them!

Larry: YEAH. And that's not even COUNTING the ones in my ARMS!

Doctor: So, what HAPPENED?

Larry: NOTHIN', really. Just a PORCUPINE.

Doctor: A PORCUPINE? Son, to get THIS many wounds, you'd have to PICK UP a porcupine with your BARE HANDS and...HUG it!

Larry: RIGHT! How'd you KNOW?

Doctor: You mean you...?

Larry: SURE. Over at the ZOO. They got some GREAT porcupines there. I just SNEAK into the CAGE, PICK one UP... and, for SOME reason, those

CHEST PAINS start again. I mean, it feels like I'm gonna DIE!

Doctor: You HUG PORCUPINES? Why would you want to do a thing like THAT?

Larry: (*Shrugging*) HEY, I'm just INTO that. I LIKE PORCUPINES.

Doctor: But HUGGING porcupines isn't GOOD for you, Larry. They're DANGEROUS! They can STICK you full of QUILLS!

Larry: SO? Don't KNOCK it until you've TRIED it!

Doctor: I don't HAVE to try it! All I have to do is look at YOU! Now, Larry…you've got to PROMISE me you'll stay away from PORCUPINES!

Larry: HEY! Are you a HEART SPECIALIST or NOT?

Doctor: 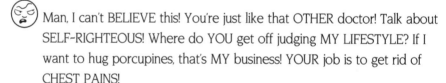 Of COURSE, but—

Larry: Well, I've got CHEST PAINS. What are you gonna DO about it?

Doctor: There's nothing I CAN do, unless you give up HUGGING PORCUPINES!

Larry:  Man, I can't BELIEVE this! You're just like that OTHER doctor! Talk about SELF-RIGHTEOUS! Where do YOU get off judging MY LIFESTYLE? If I want to hug porcupines, that's MY business! YOUR job is to get rid of CHEST PAINS!

Doctor: But—

Larry: So do a HEART thing! Whadda I NEED, OPEN HEART SURGERY? A HEART TRANSPLANT?

Doctor: No, I think you need…a DIFFERENT KIND OF DOCTOR.

Larry: Oh, YEAH? WHAT kind?

Doctor: There's a very good one NEXT DOOR. I'll just write you a REFERRAL…

Larry: I said, what KIND of doctor IS he?

Doctor: Well, he's a…PSYCHOLOGIST. He can help you figure out why you keep…HUGGING PORCUPINES.

Larry: A SHRINK? No WAY, man! (*Stands.*) You people are all ALIKE! Trying to CRUSH my ALTERNATIVE LIFESTYLE; imposing your WORN-OUT MORALITY! (*Picks up his jacket.*)

Doctor: Now, LISTEN. In MY OPINION, you need a DIFFERENT kind of TREATMENT. You need—

Larry: HEY, that's IT!

Doctor: WHAT'S it?

Larry: You're absolutely RIGHT, Doc! I DO need a different kind of treatment!

Doctor: Well, I'm GLAD you—

Larry: I don't need a HEART SPECIALIST! What I REALLY need is lots and lots of... (*Pauses to look down at his shirt.*) ACUPUNCTURE! (*Pauses.*) THANKS, Doc! You're OK, AFTER all! (*Exits.*)

Doctor: (*After a pause*) I think I'LL go to the guy next door! (*Exits, shaking head.*)

▶ For Post-Play Pondering:

1. What "diagnosis" would you give Larry? What kind of "heart specialist" did he really need?

2. What are some lifestyle choices kids at your school make that can cause them trouble?

3. When is a lifestyle choice a matter of taste, and when is it a matter of right and wrong? How do you know?

4. What might each of the following choices cost the person who makes it: (a) praying before every meal, even in public; (b) piercing ears, nose, lip, tongue, and navel; (c) chewing tobacco; (d) raising a baby instead of having an abortion; (e) living a gay lifestyle?

5. If you could change your town, would you want people to be (a) less judgmental about others' lifestyles, (b) less defensive about their own lifestyles, or (c) more aware of what their lifestyles may be doing to them? Why?

Other Scriptures for Study:
Proverbs 14:12-14; John 8:1-11; Romans 1:24-27

The Witness

Topic: Telling Others About Jesus
Scripture for Study:
Luke 24:45-48

The Scene: A street corner

The Simple Setup: No set is needed. **Officer** requires a pencil and small pad of paper. **Kid** should wear casual clothes; **Officer's** costume should suggest a police uniform (blue shirt and slacks, dark tie, badge). Sound effects (brakes squealing, crash, siren) could be recorded for **off-stage helper's** use, or **helper** could improvise them vocally at an offstage microphone.

Other Options: If you can locate a real police uniform for **Officer**, so much the better.

The Characters:

  The Kid, whiny and fretful
  The Police Officer, deadpan and skeptical

▼ ▼ ▼ ▼ ▼ ▼ ▼ ▼

*(As the skit begins, **Kid** enters and walks to center stage. **Offstage helper** provides sound effects for a loud crash. **Kid** stops and looks in surprise above heads of audience members.)*

Kid: WHOA! Looks like nobody's HURT…but what a WRECK!

*(**Offstage helper** provides sound of a siren, which grows louder and then stops. **Officer** enters, holding pencil and small pad of paper.)*

Officer: EXCUSE me. Did you see what HAPPENED here?

Kid: Oh, YEAH, Officer. I saw the whole THING! *(Talking quickly)* That candied-apple-red CORVETTE came SCREAMING around the CORNER and went through the STOP sign.

*(**Officer** writes quickly, as if taking it all down.)*

Kid: That old NOVA was TOOLING up the STREET, MINDING its own BUSINESS, and the CORVETTE plowed RIGHT into the SIDE of it. WHAM!

Officer: *(Writing)* Uh-huh.

Kid: It's a WONDER nobody got KILLED! That Corvette must have been going SIXTY MILES AN HOUR, WEAVING all over the ROAD— *(Pauses)* Hey, WAIT a minute! Are you writing this down because you want me to be…a WITNESS?

Officer: (Continuing to write until further notice) Uh-huh.

Kid: A WITNESS? No WAY! I can't WITNESS! Witnessing is for OTHER people!

Officer: Uh-huh.

Kid: YOU know…people who are cut OUT for that! People who can jump right up there on the WITNESS STAND and start TALKING!

Officer: Uh-huh.

Kid: SURE, maybe those people didn't SEE this accident, but…they've probably seen OTHER ones! They could get up there and tell the jury about THEIR accidents!

Officer: Uh-huh.

Kid: Besides, NOBODY wants to hear MY story. It's not INTERESTING enough. I'll bet YOU'VE heard some GREAT ones! Maybe a really cool HEAD-ON COLLISION, or a BIG FREEWAY PILEUP. YOU could testify! You'd be a big HIT! You'd probably be on COURT TV!

Officer: Uh-huh.

Kid: Well, maybe NOT. But I can't do it! Man, I FREEZE UP when I talk to groups. Sometimes I freeze up when I talk to MYSELF! What you need is my cousin ARNIE. Now THAT guy could talk to ANYBODY about ANYTHING. He's taken classes in PUBLIC SPEAKING and DRESSING for SUCCESS!

Officer: Uh-huh.

Kid: Of course ARNIE didn't see the accident, either. But he's a GREAT SPEAKER!

Officer: Uh-huh.

Kid: Look, I can't WITNESS! I'm not an EXPERT! I don't know anything about SKID MARKS and VELOCITY! I can't quote the DRIVERS MANUAL! I didn't study TRANSPORTATION in SCHOOL!

Officer: Uh-huh.

Kid: I…I tell you WHAT. I'll do something BETTER than witnessing. I'll print up a little PAMPHLET that talks about ACCIDENTS and has lots of QUOTES from the DRIVERS MANUAL. Then YOU can stand on a STREET CORNER and PASS IT OUT to people as they go BY.

Officer: Uh-huh.

Kid: Well, how about if I PAY somebody to go on the witness stand and testify FOR me? Maybe a whole BUNCH of us who don't want to witness could POOL our MONEY and HIRE a person like that...

Officer: Uh-huh.

Kid: Look, nobody CARES what I saw! The two DRIVERS already have their MINDS made UP about who's to BLAME!

Officer: Uh-huh.

Kid: Besides, I've never even MET the judge and jury! I'd have to spend YEARS getting to KNOW them before I could EVER talk to them about something as PERSONAL as this ACCIDENT!

Officer: Uh-huh.

Kid: OK, OK! The REAL reason I can't witness is that I don't want people to make FUN of me! I'd get up there to tell my STORY, and some LAWYER would make MINCEMEAT out of me. He'd say I didn't know what I was TALKING about. He'd EMBARRASS me in front of EVERYBODY. He'd say I was a HYPOCRITE because I'd gotten a few traffic tickets MYSELF!

Officer: Uh-huh.

Kid: Come ON, officer. Give me a BREAK. Why are you HASSLING me to WITNESS?

Officer: (*Stops writing.*) EXCUSE me...but you already ARE a witness.

Kid: HUH? Isn't a WITNESS somebody who TELLS about something?

Officer: A witness is a person who WITNESSES something. SEES it. Is THERE when it HAPPENS.

Kid: But...THAT means when I WITNESSED the ACCIDENT, I became...a WITNESS. Oh, MAN. (*Pauses*) Officer, couldn't you just...EXCUSE me?

Officer: EXCUSE me?

Kid: No, excuse ME! Excuse me from having to TELL anybody about what I've already WITNESSED!

Officer: (*Writing again*) Uh-huh.

Kid: REALLY? Boy, is THAT a RELIEF! Let's just forget about the whole—

(**Offstage helper** *provides sound of squealing brakes followed by a loud crash.* **Kid** *and* **Officer** *look above heads of audience.*)

Kid: Hey! That was MY CAR! That guy just ran into MY CAR! And now he's driving AWAY!

Officer: Uh-huh.

Kid: Well, aren't you going AFTER him?

Officer: Nope.

Kid: Why NOT?

Officer: Too SCARY. (*Pauses.*) I'm sure you UNDERSTAND.

Kid: But—

Officer: Well, I'll be moving ALONG now. Have a nice DAY. (*Exits.*)

Kid: (*Calling after* **Officer**) A NICE DAY? How can I have a NICE DAY? (*Pauses, then to audience*) I don't GET it! How can you let a little FEAR keep you from doing what you KNOW is RIGHT? (*Exits, opposite direction, in a huff.*)

For Post-Play Pondering:

1. Do people in your church ever talk about being a witness or giving testimony? What do Christians often mean by these terms?

2. How were Kid's excuses in the skit like the reasons people give for not talking about their faith? Which ones do you identify with?

3. Which do you think would be more scary: testifying about a car wreck in court, or telling a friend about Jesus? Why?

4. When it comes to knowing Jesus, what events have you "witnessed" that you could tell others about? To which events are you probably the only witness?

5. If it's true that you're already a witness in the "case" of Christianity, which of the following best describes you: (a) hostile witness, (b) star witness, (c) surprise witness, or (d) a witness taking the Fifth Amendment so that you don't have to "incriminate" yourself? Explain.

Other Scriptures for Study:

John 9:13-25; Acts 1:8; 1 Peter 3:15-16

Routine Maintenance

Topic: Friendship
Scripture for Study:
Ephesians 4:25–27

The Scene: A driveway

The Simple Setup: No set is needed. Both actors may wear casual clothes. **Kid 2** will need a large cardboard box as a prop. For the "electrical zap," use a recorded sound effect or have a helper produce it vocally at an offstage microphone.

Other Options: When the actors are "shocked" by the battery, you may want to have a helper flash the room lights off and on a few times.

The Characters:
    Kid 1, a teenage car buff
    Kid 2, friend of **Kid 1**

*(As the skit begins, the stage is empty. After a few moments, **Kids 1** and **2** enter. **Kid 2** carries a large cardboard box.)*

Kid 1:   So…got everything we NEED?

Kid 2:   *(Looking in box and speaking quickly)* Let's SEE…ANTIFREEZE, MOTOR oil, WINDSHIELD washer fluid, TRANSMISSION fluid, BRAKE fluid, SPARK plugs, AIR filter, WIPER blades, OIL filter, FUEL filter, CAR wax…and PEP-PERONI.

Kid 1:   PEPPERONI? We're doing ROUTINE MAINTENANCE on the CAR, not making PIZZA!

Kid 2:   Just KIDDING, good buddy!

Kid 1:   Oh, you crazy NUT! What would I do WITHOUT you?

Kid 2:   I don't KNOW, pal! Good thing we'll never have to FIND OUT, eh?

Kid 1:   You BET! Let's start on the CAR, my friend!

Kid 2:   *(As if ushering **Kid 1** toward imaginary car, center stage)* After YOU!

Kid 1:   *(Looking at imaginary car)* She's a BEAUTY, ISN'T she?

Kid 2:   YEAH. That was a GREAT IDEA, saving up our money to buy a car TOGETHER.

Kid 1: We SPLIT the COST, RIGHT down the MIDDLE!

Kid 2: FIFTY-FIFTY!

Kid 1: EQUAL PARTNERS!

Kid 2: SHARE and SHARE ALIKE!

Kid 1: Not everybody could DO that, you know.

Kid 2: Some people would FIGHT over it.

Kid 1: Not US.

Kid 2: We're like the TWO MUSKETEERS.

Kid 1: ONE for TWO and TWO for ONE!

Kid 2: BUDS until the BITTER END!

Kid 1: That's 'cause we know the SECRET of TRUE FRIENDSHIP.

Kid 2: That's RIGHT! (*Pauses.*) Uh...what WAS it, again?

Kid 1: ROUTINE MAINTENANCE! Just like taking care of a CAR—you've got to WORK on a friendship to keep it running SMOOTHLY!

Kid 2: Oh, YEAH.

Kid 1: You've got to keep your relationship COOL, like with ANTIFREEZE!

Kid 2: You've got to use FORGIVENESS the way a car uses OIL—to REDUCE FRICTION!

Kid 1: Keep your PRIORITIES in ALIGNMENT!

Kid 2: Make sure your GIVING AND TAKING are BALANCED, like the WHEELS!

Kid 1: Never let the PRESSURE get too HIGH, like with the TIRES!

Kid 2: And...uh...like you always EMPTY the CHEWING GUM out of the ASHTRAYS...you empty...CHEWED STUFF...out of a FRIENDSHIP...

Kid 1: Uh...RIGHT. Maybe we'd better get to work on the CAR, OK?

Kid 2: CHECK!

*(**Kid 1** pantomimes lifting the imaginary hood.)*

Kid 1: *(Pretending to check the oil)* CHECKING the OIL!

Kid 2: CHECK!

Kid 1: DOWN a quart!

Kid 2: *(Handing over imaginary oil from the box)* CHECK!

Kid 1: *(Looking at imaginary oil)* WAIT a minute! This is 5W30! We need 10W30! You brought the WRONG OIL! How could you DO such a STUPID—

Kid 2: Uh-uh-UH! Remember, ROUTINE MAINTENANCE!

Kid 1: Oh. Right. No PROBLEM, pal! ANYBODY can make a MISTAKE. We'll do the ANTIFREEZE instead.

Kid 2: CHECKING the ANTIFREEZE!

Kid 1: HALF FULL!

Kid 2: *(Standing close to **Kid 1**, handing over imaginary jug of antifreeze from the box)* Here you GO!

Kid 1: THANKS, buddy! *(Pantomimes pouring antifreeze under "hood.")*

Kid 2: HEY! You're splashing it all over my PANTS! WATCH it, you—

Kid 1: Uh-uh-UH! Remember, ROUTINE MAINTENANCE!

Kid 2: *(Through clenched teeth)* YEAH! No HARM DONE, pal! At least my PANTS will stay COOL AS A CUCUMBER…and JUST AS GREEN!

Kid 1: Let's scrape the CORROSION off these BATTERY TERMINALS. *(Reaches into box and pretends to take out screwdriver.)* I'll use THIS screwdriver. You use THAT one.

Kid 2: *(Taking out imaginary screwdriver)* OK!

*(**Kids 1** and **2** start pretending to work on imaginary battery under "hood.")*

Kid 1: Just be sure the screwdrivers don't TOUCH each—

(**Offstage helper** *provides electrical zap sound effect.*)

Kids 1 and 2: (*Together, shaking violently as if getting a big electrical shock*) AAUUGGHH!

Kid 1: (*After a pause*) You clumsy IDIOT!

Kid 2: You MORON! You could have KILLED us!

Kid 1: (*Through clenched teeth*) REMEMBER…ROUTINE…MAINTENANCE…

Kid 2: (*Through clenched teeth*) MUST…MAINTAIN…FRIENDSHIP…

Kid 1: OK…OK. Let's just FORGET working on the car right now.

Kid 2: YES. It's making us a little…TENSE.

Kid 1: I'm sure the car will do FINE for another HUNDRED MILES or so.

Kid 2: Just long enough for me to use it for my DATE tonight.

Kid 1: You can't DO that! I'M using it tonight!

Kid 2: We take TURNS! And it's MY TURN!

Kid 1: It is NOT! You had it LAST week!

Kid 2: And you had it for TWO weeks before THAT!

Kid 1: You CHEATER! I oughtta—

Kid 2: Now, now! Remember, FRIENDSHIP is like a CAR!

Kid 1: RIGHT! That's why I'm about to THROTTLE you!

Kid 2: YEAH? Well, I'm going to EMERGENCY BRAKE your neck! (*Picks up box.*) I'm taking my stuff and LEAVING! You can have YOUR half of the car…the REAR END! (**Kid 2** *exits.*)

Kid 1: (*Calling after **Kid 2***) YEAH? Well…(*After a pause, to audience*) HEY, it's not MY fault! This friendship just turned out to be…a LEMON! (*Exits.*)

For Post-Play Pondering:

1. Do you think a good friendship needs "routine maintenance," or should it run smoothly all by itself? Explain.

2. What relationship in your life has required the most work? Why?

3. How does forgiveness keep a friendship going? What's one thing for which a friend has forgiven you?

4. Read Ephesians 4:26. How many "angry sundowns" do you think a friendship can survive? Why?

5. How is friendship like (and unlike) each of the following: (a) owning a pet, (b) playing tennis, (c) using a yo-yo?

Other Scriptures for Study:

1 Samuel 20; Proverbs 17:17; 1 Corinthians 13:4-7

The Guidance Counselor

Topic: Guidance
Scripture for Study:
Psalm 25:4-15

The Scene: An office at school

The Simple Setup: You'll need a desk (or a table representing one) and chair, and a second chair for **Dana**. Set an unplugged telephone on the desk. Have **Mr. Pathfinder** wear office attire; **Dana** should wear school clothes. Props: a few sheets of paper, a newspaper, two fortune cookies in a bag, and a folding board from a board game. **Dana** can make the knocking sound offstage before entering.

Other Options: To further identify the setting, add office accessories (IN and OUT baskets, stack of papers, and pen set, for example) to the desk; you could also make or buy a poster with a message such as "Follow Your Dreams" and put it on the wall.

The Characters:

Mr. Pathfinder, school guidance counselor
Dana, a student looking for direction

▼　▼　▼　▼　▼　▼　▼　▼

(*As the skit begins,* **Mr. Pathfinder** *sits at his desk, facing the audience, shuffling papers.* **Dana** *makes knocking sound offstage.*)

Pathfinder:　Come IN!

(**Dana** *enters hesitantly.*)

Dana:　Mr. PATHFINDER?

Pathfinder:　YES?

Dana:　I...I had some QUESTIONS, and since you're the school GUIDANCE COUNSELOR...

Pathfinder:　Say no MORE! Meeting your needs for PERSONAL GUIDANCE is why I'm HERE! Have a SEAT...uh...MICHELLE, isn't it?

Dana:　No...

Pathfinder:　CALISTA?

Dana:　No...

Pathfinder: CARMEN? JENNIFER? GWYNETH? FELICITY?

Dana: Actually, it's DANA.

Pathfinder: YES. Well, it's a BIG SCHOOL. Now, what can I HELP you with, Diane?

Dana: Um…I need some DIRECTION on choosing a CAREER…a COLLEGE…a MAJOR…I just don't know which way to GO.

Pathfinder: Of COURSE you don't! But you've come to the right PLACE, Deena. I'll give you the guidance you so desperately NEED. (*Picks up newspaper and turns pages.*) Now, what is your BIRTHDAY?

Dana: Uh…April 24th.

Pathfinder: (*Consulting page of paper*) AHA! Then you are a TAURUS.

Dana: I'm…a CAR?

Pathfinder: NO, no. Taurus the BULL. Your sign of the ZODIAC. For your HOROSCOPE.

Dana: HOROSCOPE? But—

Pathfinder: Now, as a TAURUS, you are STUBBORN, FIRM, and DECISIVE. You make up your mind in a FLASH! So when it comes to these questions about your FUTURE, just…MAKE UP YOUR MIND!

Dana: But I'm not like that at ALL. I don't know what to DO. I need…GUIDANCE!

Pathfinder: Hmm. (*Puts newspaper down.*) OK, FORGET the HOROSCOPE. Let's use a much more RELIABLE, SCIENTIFIC approach. (*Reaches into a bag on the desk and takes out a fortune cookie.*) HERE. Open THIS.

Dana: What IS it?

Pathfinder: A FORTUNE COOKIE.

Dana: FORTUNE COOKIE? But that's not—

Pathfinder: Now, DARLA…are you suggesting that EASTERN WAYS OF THOUGHT have nothing to TEACH us about the GREAT QUESTIONS of LIFE?

Dana: NO, but—

Pathfinder: GOOD. Now, OPEN the COOKIE, and you'll find the ANSWER you seek.

(**Dana** *opens the cookie and takes out the slip of paper.*)

Dana: (*Reading*) "He who laughs LAST...laughs after everybody ELSE is finished LAUGHING." What's THAT supposed to mean?

Pathfinder: Uh...I don't KNOW. Try ANOTHER one. (*Hands over another fortune cookie, which **Dana** opens.*)

Dana: (*Reading*) "A journey of a THOUSAND MILES begins with TYING YOUR SHOES." What does THAT mean?

Pathfinder: AH, now we're GETTING somewhere. It means that as you begin your CAREER JOURNEY, you must PROPERLY PREPARE!

Dana: I KNOW! But HOW am I supposed to prepare?

Pathfinder: Uh...FORGET the FORTUNE COOKIES. We'll have to bring in the BIG GUNS on THIS one. (*Picks up telephone and starts dialing.*)

Dana: Who are you CALLING?

Pathfinder: The PSYCHIC FRAUDS HOT LINE! Only TWENTY DOLLARS A MINUTE.

Dana: A PSYCHIC HOTLINE? But what good is—

Pathfinder: Keep an OPEN MIND, Doreen. I always do. Why, the Psychic Frauds Hot Line helped me find my CAR KEYS once! Said to look on my KEY RING, and there they WERE!

Dana: AMAZING.

Pathfinder: And ANOTHER time they predicted the SUN would come UP in the MORNING! Talk about SOUND GUIDANCE! (*Pauses, as if listening to phone.*) UNFORTUNATELY, the LINE is busy. (*Hangs up.*)

Dana: Too BAD.

Pathfinder: All RIGHT, Donna. There's only ONE WAY to TRULY help you. (*Opens game board on desk.*) We'll ask the OUIJA BOARD.

Dana: OUIJA BOARD? But THAT'S not going to—

Pathfinder: (*Moving his finger around the board*) Clear your MIND, Diana. The SPIRITS are about to SPEAK! Let's see what MESSAGE they spell...(*Reading one letter at a time*) B...L...I...G...D...O...O...E...Y...

Dana: That spells..."BLIGDOOEY."

Pathfinder: Yes, yes..."BLIGDOOEY." (*Pauses.*) "BLIGDOOEY"? What's THAT supposed to mean?

Dana: I don't KNOW. But I don't believe in OUIJA BOARDS...or PSYCHIC HOT LINES, or FORTUNE COOKIES, or HOROSCOPES. I came here for GUIDANCE, not..."BLIGDOOEY"!

Pathfinder: Now, DORITA, I—

Dana: I'm going to do what I SHOULD have done in the FIRST place. I'm going to ask GOD for guidance.

Pathfinder: Ask GOD? Why would you want advice from an ALL-KNOWING SUPREME BEING? Use your COMMON SENSE, Danielle! Do something LOGICAL! FLIP A COIN!

Dana: (*Standing*) SORRY, Mr. Pathfinder. I've got to GO. I have some PRAYING to do.

Pathfinder: PRAYING! Not on the SCHOOL GROUNDS, I hope, Dorothy!

Dana: Oh, and ONE MORE THING. It's DANA. (*She exits.*)

Pathfinder: (*After a pause*) YES. Well...(*Looks at watch.*) LUNCH TIME! (*Stands.*) Off to the CAFETERIA! But should I have the TUNA FISH TACO...or the GOPHER WITH GRAVY? I can't DECIDE! (*Starts to leave.*) Oh, I need GUIDANCE! Perhaps if I do "ONE POTATO, TWO POTATO"...or "ROCK, PAPER, SCISSORS"...(*Exits.*)

For Post-Play Pondering:

1. Where would most kids you know go for guidance on the following questions: (a) whether to take chemistry class, (b) whether to get an abortion, (c) whether to join the military?

2. How would you rank the following sources of guidance in order from least reliable to most reliable: (a) the Internet, (b) your friends, (c) the Bible, (d) magazine advice columnists, (e) your parents? Why?

3. Would you consult a horoscope, fortune cookie, psychic hotline, or Ouija board for real advice? for fun? Why or why not?

4. About how many times did you pray for guidance in the last year? What does that say about your attitude toward God's advice?

5. Finish this sentence: "It would be a lot easier to ask for God's guidance if..."

Other Scriptures for Study:

Leviticus 19:26, 31; Proverbs 3:5-6; John 16:13-15

Screamers

Topic: Getting Along in the Group
Scripture for Study:
James 4:1-3, 11-12

The Scene: A meeting room at a youth retreat

The Simple Setup: For this spoof of teen horror movies, such as *Scream*, place four chairs center stage, more or less facing the audience. Have an **offstage helper** provide the "thunder" sound by playing a recorded sound effect—or shaking a piece of sheet metal next to an offstage microphone. If possible, have your helper flash the room lights off and on to indicate lightning. All actors should wear casual clothes—except **Person in Mask**, who should dress in black and wear a light-colored mask (a ghostly face like the one in *Scream*, a "Jason"-style hockey mask, a skull, or something similar). Give **Person in Mask** a large toy knife made of rubber or plastic.

Other Options: If you have sufficient control over your lighting, try bathing the stage in an "eerie" blue light.

The Characters:
    Snitley, nervous teenage girl
    Hater, sarcastic teenage girl
    Bully, Snitley's hunky boyfriend
    Rancid, talkative video store clerk
    Person in Mask

*(As the skit begins, **Snitley, Hater, Bully,** and **Rancid** are sitting in chairs, looking around nervously. **Snitley** and **Bully** sit next to each other. **Offstage helper** provides sound of thunder, flashes the lights on and off, then leaves the lights on.)*

Snitley: Listen to that THUNDER!

Bully: It's not the THUNDER that gets me…it's the LIGHTNING!

Hater: This is the SCARIEST YOUTH GROUP RETREAT I've ever been ON!

Rancid: YEAH, thanks to…the BACK-STABBER!

Snitley: Oh, RANCID—don't TALK about him! I'm SCARED ENOUGH as it IS! BULLY…put your ARM around me, WILL you?

Bully: *(Putting his arm around her)* It's OK, Snitley. You're SAFE with ME.

Hater: SAFE? Nobody's safe HERE! Don't you remember what's been going ON for the last TWENTY-FOUR HOURS? First it was SNARKY…then

SNIDELANDER...then TRAITOR. All of them...STABBED IN THE BACK!

Snitley: This used to be a PRETTY BIG YOUTH GROUP. But ONE by ONE, they've all been CUT DOWN. Now they're GONE! GONE!

Hater: Then it was CRABNY...then TURNCOAT...then MACK the KNIFE...

Bully: STOP it, Hater! You're just making it WORSE! We'll be OK if we just STICK TOGETHER!

Hater: STICK TOGETHER? Oh, SURE! That way the back-stabber won't have to go LOOKING for us! He can just SLICE and DICE us like FISH in a BARREL! (*Stands.*) Well, I'M not WAITING AROUND for THAT. I'm getting OUT of here! (*Starts to leave.*)

Rancid: Are you CRAZY? Haven't you ever seen a SCARY YOUTH GROUP MOVIE? All you have to do is say, "I'm getting OUT of here," and the minute you LEAVE, you're HISTORY! It happens every TIME!

Snitley: He's RIGHT, Hater! If you go out that DOOR, we'll never SEE you again!

(*Frowning,* **Hater** *returns to her chair.*)

Hater: This is RIDICULOUS. We could have gotten HELP by now if the STORM hadn't knocked out all the PHONES.

Rancid: Haven't you ever seen a SCARY YOUTH GROUP MOVIE? There's ALWAYS a storm, and it ALWAYS knocks out the phones! Why, I remember in NIGHTMARE ON CHURCH STREET—

Hater: Oh, SHUT UP, Captain Video! Why don't you go LOSE A TRIVIA CONTEST or something?

Snitley: (*After a pause*) I...I wonder who it IS.

Bully: WHO?

Snitley: The...the BACK-STABBER. It could be one of US! The back-stabber could be RIGHT HERE in this ROOM!

Rancid: No WAY! Haven't you ever seen a SCARY YOUTH GROUP MOVIE? It's always a guy wearing a MASK and dressed all in BLACK, carrying a big KNIFE! Look AROUND! Do you SEE anybody like that? Of COURSE not! Now, in the TEXAS POTLUCK MASSACRE—

Bully: Put a CORK in it, you GEEK!

Rancid: (*Standing*) Oh, so now I'm a GEEK, am I? Well, LISTEN, Mr. Football Hero, maybe I should tell everybody what you told ME at LAST year's retreat—about you and HATER!

Bully: (*Standing*) You WOULDN'T!

Snitley: (*Standing, to* **Bully**) What ABOUT you and Hater?

Bully: (*Holding his back as if in pain*) OW! (*To* **Rancid**) That was supposed to be a SECRET! You…you BACK-STABBER! (**Bully** *staggers, still holding his back.*)

Hater: (*Standing, to* **Rancid**) Leave him ALONE, twerp! Or should I tell everyone what you PRAYED FOR in our SMALL GROUP last week?

Rancid: (*Holding his back as if in pain*) NO! PLEASE!

Hater: You prayed that somebody would go OUT with you even though you're such a NERD!

Rancid: OWW! Stab me in the BACK, why don't you? (*He staggers, clutching his back.*)

Snitley: (*Holding her back, to* **Bully**) You…you went OUT with HATER? I thought you LOVED me…and now you've STABBED ME IN THE BACK!

Bully: (*Falling to his knees in pain*) Oh, GROW UP! Besides, she means NOTHING to me! NOTHING!

Hater: (*Grabbing her back in pain, to* **Bully**) NOTHING? OWW! How can you STAB ME IN THE BACK like that?

(*They all fall to their hands and knees, groaning in pain.*)

Snitley: So…YOU'RE the back-stabber! (*She collapses as if dead.*)

Bully: No, YOU are! (*He collapses as if dead.*)

Hater: No, YOU are! (*She collapses as if dead.*)

Rancid: Don't you SEE? We're ALL the back-stabbers! It's just like…in that MOVIE…(*He collapses as if dead.*)

(*For a few moments there is a pause. Then **offstage helper** provides thunder sound effect. Suddenly, **Person in Mask** enters, brandishing a large toy knife and screaming like a maniac.*)

Person in Mask: AARRGGHH! (*Getting no reaction,* **Person in Mask** *looks around at "corpses" on floor, then sighs.*) What IS it with these YOUTH GROUPS? By the time I get there…they've always FINISHED THE JOB!

(**Person in Mask** *shrugs and exits.* **Offstage helper** *provides thunder sound effect then flashes the lights off, on, and off.*)

For Post-Play Pondering:

1. When it comes to relationships, what does it mean to be a "back-stabber"? Have you ever felt as if someone had "stabbed you in the back"?

2. Which do you think is worse: back-stabbing, grudges, or gossip? Why?

3. How could back-stabbing, grudges, and gossip affect a group like ours? On a scale of one to ten (ten being "big problem"), how would you rate our group in those three areas?

4. Is back-stabbing a problem we should just put up with in our group? If not, how should we deal with it?

5. If you had to design a youth group retreat that would help us learn to get along better, what three activities would you most want to include? Why?

Other Scriptures for Study:
Proverbs 26:20-22; 1 Corinthians 11:17-22, 33-34; 1 Peter 3:8-12

Just Be Careful

Topic: Premarital Sex
Scripture for Study:
Titus 2:6, 11-14

The Scene: A classroom

The Simple Setup: No set is needed. Have **Ms. Tuffnagel** wear a "teacher" outfit; **Kids** can wear school clothes. Before the skit, "plant" three **Kids** in the audience.

Other Options: To further identify the setting, place a chalkboard behind **Ms. Tuffnagel**.

The Characters:

    Ms. Tuffnagel, hard-as-nails health teacher
    Kid 1
    Kid 2
    Kid 3

▼ ▼ ▼ ▼ ▼ ▼ ▼ ▼

*(As the skit begins, **Kids 1, 2,** and **3** are "planted" in the audience. **Ms. Tuffnagel** enters and stands center stage.)*

Tuffnagel:		All RIGHT, people! Settle DOWN! This is a HEALTH CLASS, not a HOCKEY GAME!
Kid 1:		*(Raises hand.)* Ms. TUFFNAGEL?
Tuffnagel:		YES?
Kid 1:		Is THIS the day when we talk about…YOU know?
Tuffnagel:		YES, yes. And I don't want any SNICKERING! This is a PERFECTLY NORMAL part of EVERYONE'S LIFE. If you feel FIDGETY dealing with this subject, just get OVER it!
Kid 2:		*(Raising hand)* Uh…Ms. TUFFNAGEL?
Tuffnagel:		YEAH?
Kid 2:		Will this be on the TEST?
Tuffnagel:		You BET it will! So listen CAREFULLY, and take NOTES! *(Pauses.)* OK! Today we discuss that topic you've always WONDERED about. I'm talking about that LITTLE WORD that starts with S. I'm talking about…SUICIDE!
Kid 3:		*(Raising hand)* Uh…Ms. TUFFNAGEL?

Tuffnagel: WHAT?

Kid 3: I thought we were going to discuss...SOMETHING ELSE.

Tuffnagel: Something ELSE? What else could it BE? It starts with S, you're all CURIOUS about it, and talking about it makes people UNCOMFORTABLE. Of COURSE, it's suicide! (*Pauses.*) Now, some of your PARENTS probably don't want you to hear what I'm going to SAY today. But so WHAT? They're stuck back in the 1950s. They think kids still care about stuff like SPORTS and HAMBURGERS and CARS. They don't understand that what you're REALLY thinking about every MINUTE, TWENTY-FOUR HOURS A DAY, is...SUICIDE!

Kid 1: (*Raising hand*) Ms. TUFFNAGEL?

Tuffnagel: HUH?

Kid 1: I don't think about suicide all the time.

Tuffnagel: Oh, yeah, SURE! Everybody KNOWS that's all kids think about! And why WOULDN'T you? Everywhere you LOOK, you're BOMBARDED with it. TV SHOWS about people KILLING themselves...ROCK MUSIC about ENDING IT ALL...It's in the NEWSPAPERS, MAGAZINES, the INTERNET...No WONDER you're obsessed with it!

Kid 2: (*Raising hand*) Ms. TUFFNAGEL?

Tuffnagel: What IS it?

Kid 2: I'M not obsessed with suicide.

Tuffnagel: Then you're not NORMAL! EVERY teenager is FULL of SELF-DESTRUCTIVE URGES! You can't HELP it! All your FRIENDS are doing it! And that's why I'm here to tell you how to practice...SAFE SUICIDE!

Kid 3: (*Raising hand*) Uh...Ms. TUFFNAGEL?

Tuffnagel: What NOW?

Kid 3: SAFE SUICIDE? Wouldn't it be better to just...ABSTAIN?

Tuffnagel: ABSTAIN? What planet are YOU from? EVERYBODY KNOWS teenagers can't CONTROL themselves! You're all going to kill yourselves ANYWAY, so you may as well do it RESPONSIBLY!

Kid 1: (*Raising hand*) Um...Ms. TUFFNAGEL?

Tuffnagel: WHAT? WHAT?

Kid 1: I don't want to kill myself.

Tuffnagel: Fine, FINE. You're just not READY, that's all. You're AFRAID. You're IMMATURE. Wait until you're READY. Don't let anybody RUSH you into it. You'll KNOW when it's time.

Kid 1: But I thought there's only ONE right time for your life to end—when GOD says it's time.

Tuffnagel: Oh, GREAT! A RELIGIOUS WACKO! Stop trying to impose your WEIRD PERSONAL BELIEFS on the REST of us!

Kid 1: But—

Tuffnagel: No more INTERRUPTIONS! On to SAFE SUICIDE! Now, KILLING YOURSELF can be RISKY BUSINESS these days. HANGING, POISON, DRIVING YOUR CAR INTO A TREE—they're all MESSY and INCONVENIENT. So at the END of CLASS, I'll be passing out THIRTY-CALIBER PISTOLS you can use to SHOOT yourselves. If you need EXTRA BULLETS, just ask the SCHOOL NURSE. Any QUESTIONS?

Kid 2: Uh...Ms. Tuffnagel...are you ENCOURAGING us to commit suicide?

Tuffnagel: ENCOURAGING you? Of COURSE not! Becoming SUICIDALLY ACTIVE is a very PERSONAL decision. You should talk it over with people you can TRUST—people about to JUMP OFF BRIDGES, people who like to CUT THEIR WRISTS, people who are SITTING IN CARS IN GARAGES WITH THE ENGINES RUNNING...ANYBODY but PARENTS and CHURCH-GOERS, because they always say NO. (*Pauses.*) Time's UP! Any more QUESTIONS?

Kid 3: Ms. Tuffnagel...is there any HOMEWORK?

Tuffnagel: 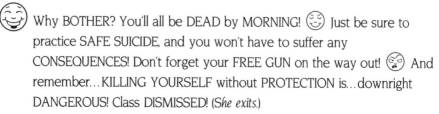 Why BOTHER? You'll all be DEAD by MORNING! Just be sure to practice SAFE SUICIDE, and you won't have to suffer any CONSEQUENCES! Don't forget your FREE GUN on the way out! And remember...KILLING YOURSELF without PROTECTION is...downright DANGEROUS! Class DISMISSED! (*She exits.*)

► For Post-Play Pondering:

1. What was this skit really about? How do you know?

2. Do you agree or disagree with the following statements: (a) "Teenagers think about sex all the time"; (b) "When it comes to sex, teenagers can't control themselves"?

3. How is Ms. Tuffnagel's safe-suicide lesson like the approach taken to sex education in your school? How is it different?

4. What does "safe sex" protect a person from? What does it not protect a person from?

5. If you have children someday, what will you tell them about the right-and-wrong aspect of pre-marital sex? Why?

Other Scriptures for Study:

Proverbs 5; Ephesians 5:3; 1 Thessalonians 4:3-8; Hebrews 13:4

The Plymouth Rock Cafe

Topic: Being Thankful
Scripture for Study:
Colossians 3:15-17

The Scene: A restaurant In Plymouth, Massachusetts, 1623

The Simple Setup: At center stage, place a table with three chairs around it. Props: Three cardboard menus that say "Plymouth Rock Cafe"; pencil and small pad of paper for **Server**; basket covered with a cloth napkin. For costumes, do what you can to make the actors look like "Thanksgiving pilgrims." For the guys, this would mean white shirts, black pants, and black construction-paper "pilgrim hats"; for **Hester** (and **Server**, if played by a girl), black dress and white bonnet.

Other Options: If you have time (and a helper with sewing skills), look up Puritan clothing in an encyclopedia or other reference and add details that make the costumes look more authentic.

The Characters:

> **Benjamin,** cranky pilgrim teenager
> **Hester,** humble pilgrim teenager
> **Jonathan,** crabby pilgrim teenager
> **Server,** matter-of-fact pilgrim teenager

*(As the skit begins, **Benjamin, Hester,** and **Jonathan** sit at a table, looking at menus labeled "Plymouth Rock Cafe." After a few moments, **Server** enters, carrying pad and pencil.)*

Server: Welcome to the PLYMOUTH ROCK CAFE. Can I take thy ORDER?

Benjamin: Yeah, I'll have a CHEESEBURGER.

Server: SORRY, the cheeseburger hath not yet been INVENTED. After all, this is the COLONY of PLYMOUTH in the YEAR OF OUR LORD 1623.

Benjamin: Don't REMIND me. What a LOUSY time to be ALIVE.

Jonathan: I'll have a LARGE ORDER of FRIES.

Server: Sorry, FRENCH FRIES hath not yet been invented. After all, this is—

Jonathan: Yeah, yeah, I KNOW. Dost thou not have ANY decent food?

Server: We have BEEF JERKY, CORN BREAD, and BUFFALO STRINGS.

Benjamin: You mean buffalo WINGS? CHICKEN, with that GOOD, SPICY SAUCE?

Server: No, I mean REALLY STRINGY PIECES OF BUFFALO. NO SAUCE.

Jonathan: YUCK!

Hester: I'll have the CORN BREAD, please.

Benjamin: Me, too.

Jonathan: Me, too.

(**Server** *pretends to write on pad, then exits.*)

Benjamin: Man, being a PILGRIM is the PITS. There's no place to get a REAL MEAL in this colony!

Hester: There will be SOON. Look out the WINDOW.

Jonathan: (*Looking over heads of audience*) WHERE?

Hester: Verily, BEHOLD! Preparations for the GREAT FEAST have begun. It is nearly the time of THANKSGIVING declared by GOVERNOR BRADFORD!

Benjamin: BRADFORD! What a DORK. Him and his HOLIDAY PROCLAMATIONS. SQUANTO DAY...MYLES STANDISH DAY...SCURVY PREVENTION WEEK...and now THIS!

Hester: But we have so much to be THANKFUL for. We have LIFE in ABUNDANCE!

Jonathan: You call this LIFE? We wear the same CLOTHES SIX days a WEEK! We have to wear these STUPID HATS! Even INDOOR PLUMBING hath not yet been invented!

Hester: Yet the Lord hath been GOOD to us. We should be THANKFUL.

Benjamin: For WHAT? CORN ON THE COB? That's all those INDIANS brought us to EAT last winter!

Hester: But, through THEM, the Lord helped us SURVIVE. They taught us to plant CORN, SQUASH, and PUMPKINS.

Jonathan: PUMPKINS? I'm SICK of pumpkins! Thee cannot EAT them; thee cannot WEAR them; thee may as well CARVE FACES on them!

Hester: Guys, the Lord meets ALL our NEEDS. Shall we FORGET his BLESSINGS?

Benjamin: BLESSINGS? Let him bless me with a DOLBY AC-3 SOUND SYSTEM with 80-watt FLOOR SPEAKERS and a SUBWOOFER! THEN I'd have something to be THANKFUL for!

Hester: A WHAT?

Benjamin: Never mind.

Hester: Perhaps all things we might WISH for have not yet been INVENTED. Even SO, in our SPIRITS we can have LIFE TO THE FULL! THAT'S what the Thanksgiving celebration is all ABOUT!

Jonathan: Aw, it's gonna be BORING. (*He points above heads of audience.*) Look at all those LITTLE OLD LADIES carrying around pans of YAMS and stuff. There's GOODY WATKINS...

Benjamin: Hey, what IS it with this "GOODY" thing, ANYWAY? We've got GOODY WATKINS, GOODY PROCTOR, GOODY TWO-SHOES... Why can't they have NORMAL names, like BRIDGET and COURTNEY?

Jonathan: And just LOOK at the MAIN COURSE! TURKEY! Whose idea was THAT? Whatever happened to PIZZA?

Benjamin: Oh, TURKEY is PERFECT! This whole CENTURY is a turkey!

Hester: (*Standing*) That's IT! I cannot ABIDE this anymore! Thy COMPLAINING is like the DRIPPING OF WATER from a LEAKY CISTERN! I'm joining the CELEBRATION. Fare thee WELL! (*She exits.*)

Benjamin: WHOA! Who put the bee in HER bonnet?

Jonathan: Aw, she just had to go for a SPIN...in her MAYFLOWER COMPACT!

(*They laugh. Enter **Server** with covered basket.*)

Server: Here's thy CORN BREAD. Enjoy thy SUP! (**Server** *puts basket on table and exits.*)

Benjamin: So...wilt thou return THANKS?

Jonathan: I did it LAST time.

Benjamin: Nay, 'twas ME!

Jonathan: Did NOT!

Benjamin: Did, TOO!

Jonathan: Did NOT!

Benjamin: Did, TOO!

Jonathan: (*Standing*) FINE! Eat all the corn bread THYSELF! May it taste like TINDER in thy BIG MOUTH! (*He exits.*)

Benjamin: (*Standing*) Oh, YEAH? Well, THOU art the real TURKEY around here, BOZO!

(**Benjamin** *exits in opposite direction. After a pause,* **Server** *enters, sees the empty table, and shakes head.*)

Server: (*Picking up basket*) And NOBODY payeth the BILL! (*Yelling offstage*) Hey, THANKS…for NOTHIN'! (**Server** *exits.*)

►For Post-Play Pondering:

1. What reasons did Hester give for being thankful? Why didn't the guys agree?

2. Do you think the Thanksgiving holiday really encourages people to thank God? Why or why not?

3. What are three things you have that someone else might be thankful to get?

4. If this skit took place in a fast-food place today, what might the kids complain about?

5. If it were illegal to thank God for what you have, would you break the law? What if the penalty were death? Explain.

Other Scriptures for Study:

Ecclesiastes 2:24-25; 1 Thessalonians 5:16-18; Hebrews 12:28-29

The Principal's Office

Topic: Guilt

Scripture for Study:
Isaiah 43:16-25

The Scene: Outside a principal's office

The Simple Setup: Place two chairs center stage, facing the audience. Both **Kids** may wear casual clothes; **Secretary** should wear business attire. Note that all roles may be played by either gender.

Other Options: To help identify the characters further, you could have **Tough Kid** wear an outfit that suggests rebellion (shirt depicting a controversial recording artist, chains, etc.) and **Weepy Kid** wear one that implies conformity and uptightness (suit, tie, etc.).

The Characters:

Tough Kid, a bragging troublemaker

Weepy Kid, a sobbing self-criticizer

Secretary, seen-it-all worker in the school office

*(As the skit begins, **Tough Kid** and **Weepy Kid** sit on chairs, center stage, facing the audience.)*

Tough Kid: SO, you got sent here to the PRINCIPAL'S OFFICE, eh? Ever been here BEFORE?

Weepy Kid: OH, yes. MANY times.

Tough Kid: Not as many as ME, I bet! Yeah, I come to see my OLD BUDDY the PRINCIPAL pretty OFTEN. My TEACHERS see to THAT.

Weepy Kid: Why are you here THIS time?

Tough Kid: Oh, just a little MISUNDERSTANDING. Something about a PAPER AIRPLANE and my ALGEBRA TEACHER'S HAIRPIECE.

Weepy Kid: HAIRPIECE?

Tough Kid: YEAH. That's what FELL OFF when I threw the PAPER AIRPLANE. Can you BELIEVE it? I was doing the guy a FAVOR! His toupee looks like a DEAD RACCOON sitting on his head!

Weepy Kid: Well, I guess he—

Tough Kid: I'm ALWAYS getting sent to the principal's office for NOTHING. Like LAST WEEK.

Weepy Kid: What HAPPENED?

Tough Kid: Aw, just a little FAILURE TO COMMUNICATE. Something about a WATER BALLOON and the JANITOR'S EYEBALLS.

Weepy Kid: EYEBALLS?

Tough Kid: YEAH. That's what POPPED OUT when I dropped the WATER BALLOON on him in the PARKING LOT. How was I supposed to know he had LOOSE EYEBALLS?

Weepy Kid: Well, maybe—

Tough Kid: And the week before THAT...I got sent here for NO REASON AT ALL. Something about a FLAME THROWER and a GRILLED CHEESE SANDWICH.

Weepy Kid: GRILLED CHEESE SANDWICH?

Tough Kid: YEAH. That's what the LIBRARIAN looked like after I pointed the FLAME THROWER and—

Weepy Kid: Never MIND. I get the PICTURE.

Tough Kid: Pretty UNFAIR, huh? Every time some MINOR UNPLEASANTNESS occurs, I get sent to the PRINCIPAL'S OFFICE! And the PUNISHMENTS! Once I had to write TWENTY-FIVE TIMES on the BOARD, 'I WILL NOT GIVE NUCLEAR WEDGIES TO MY FELLOW STUDENTS'! THAT'S when you ACTUALLY pull their SHORTS UP OVER their HEADS!

Weepy Kid: Well, I—

Tough Kid: So, who sent YOU to the principal's office? Mr. GRUMPSTEIN? Old lady PLUGUGLY? Or that CAFETERIA LADY with the HOOK?

Weepy Kid: I did.

Tough Kid: WHAT?

Weepy Kid: I sent MYSELF to the principal's office.

Tough Kid: You sent YOURSELF? Why would you do THAT?

Weepy Kid: Because I'm so BAD! I keep doing TERRIBLE THINGS, AWFUL things!

Tough Kid: WOW! Are you, like, a SERIAL KILLER or something? A CANNIBAL? A TERRORIST?

Weepy Kid: WORSE!

Tough Kid: REALLY? Like, what have you DONE?

Weepy Kid: Once I forgot to EMPTY MY MILK CARTON COMPLETELY before THROWING IT IN THE TRASH!

Tough Kid: HUH?

Weepy Kid: I know, it's UNBELIEVABLE! ANOTHER time, on a TEST where you FILL IN THOSE LITTLE CIRCLES, I used a NUMBER THREE PENCIL instead of a NUMBER TWO!

Tough Kid: Is that IT?

Weepy Kid: Oh, NO! Last month I didn't CHEER as loudly as I SHOULD have at the PEP RALLY. Then in BAND PRACTICE I accidentally played a C SHARP instead of a C NATURAL! Then I said in HISTORY class that the SIXTH PRESIDENT OF THE UNITED STATES was JOHN ADAMS!

Tough Kid: SO?

Weepy Kid: It was John QUINCY Adams!

Tough Kid: Let me get this STRAIGHT. Every time you do one of these…THINGS…you SEND YOURSELF to the PRINCIPAL'S OFFICE?

Weepy Kid: Of COURSE!

Tough Kid: WHY?

Weepy Kid: Because I feel so…GUILTY!

Tough Kid: GUILTY? What's THAT?

Weepy Kid: YOU know! That HORRIBLE, GNAWING FEELING of SHAME you get when you do something WRONG!

Tough Kid: NOPE. Doesn't ring a BELL.

Weepy Kid: It just EATS AWAY at you until you can't STAND it anymore! That's why I keep sending myself to the PRINCIPAL'S OFFICE! Because I DESERVE to be PUNISHED! Because I'm such a miserable, no-good, law-breaking WORM!

(**Secretary** *enters.*)

Secretary: OK. CHRIS?

Weepy Kid: YES?

Secretary: The principal says you can GO.

Weepy Kid: I KNEW it! I'm being EXPELLED! Oh, I'm such a ROTTEN PERSON! I don't DESERVE to LIVE!

Secretary: Uh...the principal says you can go BACK TO CLASS. You're not being EXPELLED. All you did was misspell the word "NEUTRINO" on your PHYSICS PAPER.

Weepy Kid: But I'm GUILTY! GUILTY, I tell you!

Secretary: No, you're NOT. The principal says you're ALREADY FORGIVEN. You don't have to keep SENDING YOURSELF to the OFFICE. You're FREE to GO!

Weepy Kid: (*Standing*) Oh, I get it. This is my PUNISHMENT! LIVING with the GUILT! Letting it EAT AWAY at me FOREVER! It's what I DESERVE! THANK you! THANK you! (*Exits.*)

Secretary: (*After a pause*) I'll NEVER understand that kid. (*Starts to leave.*)

Tough Kid: HEY! What about ME? Am I free to go, too?

Secretary: No WAY. The principal wants to SEE you...NOW.

Tough Kid: (*Standing*) No SWEAT. It's just a little MISUNDERSTANDING.

Secretary: Like the one about the MICROWAVE OVEN and the FOREIGN EXCHANGE STUDENT? (*Exits.*)

Tough Kid: (*Following* **Secretary**) Now, how was I supposed to know you can't make BELGIAN WAFFLES out of BELGIANS? Give me a BREAK! (*Exits.*)

▶ For Post-Play Pondering:

1. Why do you suppose some people never seem to feel guilty, while others seem to feel guilty all the time?

2. When you feel guilty, what changes do you tend to experience in your (a) stomach, (b) head, (c) relationship with God?

3. How can a person be forgiven for doing something wrong? When you hear that God has forgiven you, do you really believe it? Why or why not?

4. Can you name a time when a person *should* feel guilty? Can you name an act that isn't really a sin, but that a person might feel guilty about? How can you know the difference?

5. Next time you feel like putting yourself in "detention" because of something you've done, what should you do?

Other Scriptures for Study:

Psalm 38; Hebrews 10:1-4, 19-23; 1 John 1:9

How Do You Spell Belief?

Topic: Doubt
Scripture for Study:
Mark 9:21-24

The Scene: A street corner

The Simple Setup: No set is needed for this spoof of the classic Rolaids TV commercial. Remind your actors to say "belief" carefully so that no one mistakes it for *relief*, and to spell out the words which have hyphens between the letters. **Announcer** will need a roll of antacid tablets and a hand-held microphone (or something resembling one), and should wear a suit. The other characters may wear casual clothes.

Other Options: If you like, make a large "bottle" using a toilet paper tube and construction paper; label it "Growl-Aids" and give it to **Announcer** to use as a prop.

The Characters:
>**Announcer**, trying to act like a reporter
>**Kid 1**, nervous
>**Kid 2**, robotic
>**Kid 3**, a little too laid-back

▼   ▼   ▼   ▼   ▼   ▼   ▼   ▼

(As the skit begins, **Announcer** stands center stage, holding what looks like a microphone.)

Announcer: I'm here on a BUSY STREET CORNER, talking to people about GROWL-AIDS…the STOMACH ANTACID that helps you through those TOUGH TIMES…those times when you feel like DOUBTING YOUR FAITH.

(Enter **Kid 1**.)

Announcer: Ah, HERE'S someone we can talk to. EXCUSE me!

Kid 1: WHAT? (*Putting hands in the air*) Oh, please, DON'T SHOOT ME! Take my MONEY! No, wait, I don't HAVE any money…

Announcer: Calm DOWN! This isn't a GUN, it's a MICROPHONE.

Kid 1: Oh. (*Puts hands down.*) Well, could you give me some MONEY, then?

Announcer: NO, but I can give you this FREE SAMPLE of GROWL-AIDS, the tablet that absorbs NINE TIMES THE WEIGHT OF THE CHRYSLER BUILDING in EXCESS STOMACH ACID! (*Gives **Kid 1** the roll or "bottle" of "antacid tablets."*) Now, TELL us: How do YOU spell "BELIEF"?

Kid 1: "BELIEF"? I spell it F-E-A-R!

Announcer: F-E-A-R? Why, that spells "FEAR"! What are you so AFRAID of?

Kid 1: S-sometimes when I'm in SCIENCE CLASS and the TEACHER starts talking about EVOLUTION, I wonder whether HE'S RIGHT and the BIBLE is WRONG. (*Looks around as if expecting to be struck by lightning.*) GOD must be so MAD at me for THINKING that! He must HATE it when I d-d-d—

Announcer: DOUBT?

Kid 1: Oh, don't SAY that word! I just KNOW He's going to PUNISH me for QUESTIONING! I'd better get OUT of here before I get HIT by LIGHTNING, or a TORNADO, or a FALLING SAFE that says "ACME" on the side! (*Running out*) Please, don't SHOOT me! (*Exits.*)

Announcer: It's not a GUN, it's…oh, NEVER MIND.

(*Enter **Kid 2**.*)

Announcer: Ah, HERE'S someone else we can survey. PARDON ME!

Kid 2: Yes…can I ASSIST you in some way?

Announcer: We're talking to people about GROWL-AIDS, the tablet that absorbs NINE HUNDRED TIMES THE WEIGHT OF THE POLAR ICECAPS in EXCESS STOMACH ACID! Now, TELL me: How do YOU spell "BELIEF"?

Kid 2: "BELIEF"…I spell it M-O-M - A-N-D - D-A-D.

Announcer: Let's SEE…That spells…"MOM AND DAD."

Kid 2: CORRECT.

Announcer: Well, what do MOM and DAD have to do with BELIEF?

Kid 2: I believe whatever THEY believe.

Announcer: I SEE. And what do THEY believe?

Kid 2: I have no IDEA.

Announcer: Then how do you know whether you BELIEVE it?

Kid 2: I just DO. I don't wish to THINK about it. It is too DIFFICULT. I would rather go along with whatever THEY say and whatever the CHURCH says, even if I do not know what it IS.

Announcer: Well, do you ever DOUBT your FAITH?

Kid 2: FAITH? What is FAITH? Sorry, an ERROR of TYPE TEN occurred. REBOOT. REBOOT. (*He exits.*)

Announcer: HMM.

(*Enter* **Kid 3**.)

Announcer: Well, let's try ONE MORE. EXCUSE me!

Kid 3: HEY! What's HAPPENIN'?

Announcer: We're talking to people about GROWL-AIDS, the tablet that absorbs NINE BILLION TIMES THE WEIGHT OF THE ENTIRE SOLAR SYSTEM in EXCESS STOMACH ACID! Now, TELL me: How do YOU spell BELIEF?

Kid 3: BELIEF? How about if I spell MISSISSIPPI instead? Let's see… M-double-I…No…M-S-I-double-S-S-I…

Announcer: BELIEF! How do you spell BELIEF?

Kid 3: OK, OK! If I HAD to spell BELIEF, it would be L-A-T-E-R.

Announcer: But that spells LATER.

Kid 3: I KNOW! I'd rather not worry about that BELIEF stuff NOW. I'll just leave it UP IN THE AIR and not come down on ONE side or the OTHER. Maybe Christianity's TRUE, maybe it ISN'T. Maybe I can TRUST the Bible, maybe NOT.

Announcer: But when are you going to start THINKING about these things and making up your MIND?

Kid 3: Oh, I don't know. LATER. Maybe when I'm real OLD, like TWENTY-FIVE…or TWENTY-FIVE AND A HALF.

Announcer: But what if you don't LIVE that long? And HOW are you going to live if you don't know what you BELIEVE?

Kid 3: Good QUESTION! I'll think about it... LATER! (*Exits.*)

Announcer: I give UP! These people don't need ANTACID TABLETS...they need HOOKED ON SPELLING! (*Clears throat and composes self.*) All RIGHT. This is your PERSON ON THE STREET for GROWL-AIDS, reminding you that when you learn how to spell BELIEF, it's a real RELIEF! (*Exits.*)

For Post-Play Pondering:

1. How would you explain to a third-grader what *belief, doubt,* and *faith* mean?

2. How would you spell *belief* in a way that shows how you usually handle doubts about Christianity and the Bible?

3. What advice would you give the three kids in the skit?

4. When you have doubts about your faith, do you feel like you need (a) an antacid, (b) more information, (c) a friend, (d) forgiveness, or (e) something else?

5. How can we in this group help each other with our doubts?

Other Scriptures for Study:

Mark 11:22-24; Luke 8:4-15; Jude 20-22

Dr. Jekyll and Dr. Jekyll

Topic: Becoming a New Person
Scripture for Study:
Ezekiel 11:17-20

The Scene: A dungeon laboratory

The Simple Setup: Place a table center stage and cover it with a sheet—one that reaches the floor, if possible. Place a few clear glass or plastic containers on the table and fill them half full of water; add food coloring to make the water in each container a different hue. **Dr. Jekyll** should wear a suit that looks as old-fashioned as possible; have **Mrs. Really** wear a dark dress and apron. Props: feather duster, hand mirror, Halloween mask (put the mirror on the table, and put the mask behind the table before the skit). If your actors can use British accents, encourage them to do so. Have **Mrs. Really** provide the knocking sound offstage before she enters.

Other Options: If you have time, find glassware that looks like it belongs in a real laboratory, such as test tubes or flasks. Try a hobby shop or toy store that carries chemistry sets.

The Characters:
Dr. Jekyll, mad scientist
Mrs. Really, his housekeeper

▼ ▼ ▼ ▼ ▼ ▼ ▼ ▼

(As the skit begins, **Dr. Jekyll** works feverishly at a covered table, mixing vials of colored liquids, pouring them into each other, and sniffing them. Finally he holds one vial aloft.)

Jekyll: YES! YES! THIS is the formula that will do the TRICK! Now, if I can just determine the correct DOSAGE...

(**Mrs. Really** knocks offstage.)

Really: (From offstage) Dr. JEKYLL! Dr. JEKYLL!

Jekyll: (Putting vial down) Is that YOU, Mrs. Really?

Really: YES, sir, it's ME. I've come to DUST your SECRET LABORATORY where you do your VILE, FORBIDDEN EXPERIMENTS.

Jekyll: Oh, must you do it right NOW? I'm on the verge of a MAJOR BREAK-THROUGH!

Really: I'm afraid I MUST, sir. I'm scheduled to dust Dr. FRANKENSTEIN'S secret laboratory down the STREET in TWENTY MINUTES.

Jekyll: OH, very WELL, Mrs. Really! Come IN!

(**Mrs. Really** *enters, carrying a feather duster.*)

Really: THAT'S the way, now, Dr. Jekyll. No use having a DUSTY LABORATORY for your VILE, FORBIDDEN EXPERIMENTS. A CLEAN dungeon is a HAPPY dungeon, I always say.

Jekyll: REALLY?

Really: Yes?

Jekyll: What?

Really: You said my NAME—REALLY.

Jekyll: NO, no, I meant…never MIND.

Really: Very WELL, sir. I'll just polish a bit of GLASSWARE and be on my WAY. (*She uses feather duster on table.*)

Jekyll: FORGET the DUSTING, Mrs. Really. I have something more IMPORTANT for you to do. I want you to witness the most amazing TRANSFORMA-TION in the HISTORY of the WORLD!

Really: (*Stops dusting.*) TRANSFORMATION, sir?

Jekyll: All my LIFE I've wanted to CHANGE. I know I'm not what I OUGHT to be. I've longed to become a BRAND NEW PERSON! And now I SHALL!

Really: But HOW?

Jekyll: (*Holding up vial*) By drinking THIS! It's a formula of my OWN DESIGN, perfected through years of VILE, FORBIDDEN EXPERIMENTS! At LAST, I'm ready to take the FIRST SIP!

Really: My GOODNESS!

Jekyll: Step BACK, Mrs. Really…and behold…the TRANSFORMATION! (*He drinks from the vial and sets it on the table, then clutches at his throat.*) AAGGH! (*He sinks down, disappearing behind the table.*) ARRGGH! AAUGH! ARRGGH!!

Really: Oh, MY!

(**Jekyll** *slowly rises from behind the table, looking exactly as he did before.*)

Jekyll: AH! THAT'S better! And so you SEE, Mrs. Really, I am a DIFFERENT MAN! Completely CHANGED! Everything has become NEW!

Really: Uh...begging your PARDON, sir...

Jekyll: Yes, YES, what IS it?

Really: You look the SAME to ME, sir. Same old Dr. JEKYLL, I'd say.

Jekyll: WHAT? (*Picks up hand mirror from table and looks at himself.*) AAUUGGHH! NO! I haven't changed at ALL! (*Puts down mirror and picks up vial.*) I must have taken the wrong AMOUNT. I need TWICE as much! (*Drinks from vial and sets it down.*) WATCH, Mrs. Really! Watch as the OLD Dr. Jekyll is NO MORE! (*Clutching his throat*) ARRGH! UGGH! AAUUGHH!! (*He sinks down, disappearing behind the table.*) UNGGH! URRGGH! WHOO!

Really: HEAVENS to BETSY!

(**Jekyll** *slowly rises from behind the table, looking exactly as he did before.*)

Jekyll: THERE! CHANGED at LAST! How do you like...the NEW ME?

Really: Um...looks like the OLD me, sir. Or I SHOULD say, the old YOU.

Jekyll: WHAT? (*Picks up mirror and looks at himself.*) It CAN'T be! According to my CALCULATIONS, I should be a TOTALLY DIFFERENT PERSON! (*Puts down mirror and picks up vial.*) I'll QUADRUPLE the dosage! (*Drinks the rest of the liquid.*) That's IT! You're about to see...the NEW Dr. Jekyll! (*Clutching his throat*) OOOOH! WOWF! GLUGGH! (*He sinks down, disappearing behind the table.*) EEEE! OOF! YIPPIE–TI–YI–YAY!

Really: SAINTS ALIVE!

(**Jekyll** *slowly rises from behind the table. This time he has a Halloween mask over his head.*)

Jekyll: SUCCESS at LAST! The TRANSFORMATION is COMPLETE!

Really: Uh...no OFFENSE, sir...but that's just a HALLOWEEN MASK.

Jekyll: (*Pulling off the mask and tossing it on the table*) BLAST! How did you KNOW?

Really: You left the PRICE TAG on.

Jekyll: Oh, Mrs. REALLY! This is NEVER going to work! I'll NEVER be able to change!

Really: FRANKLY, Dr. Jekyll, I'VE always believed there's only ONE way to become a NEW PERSON.

Jekyll: What's THAT?

Really: Through the POWER of the one who MADE you in the FIRST place.

Jekyll: But THAT would be…(*Pauses as he begins to understand.*) OH!

Really: Why don't you come with ME, now, Dr. Jekyll? It's not GOOD to spend all your time in this DREARY, OLD DUNGEON.

Jekyll: BUT—

Really: (*Taking his arm*) Come ALONG, now. I know someone who could HELP.

Jekyll: You mean that FRANKENSTEIN fellow?

Really: NO, sir. Someone down at the CHURCH.

Jekyll: (*As they start to leave*) REALLY?

Really: Beg your PARDON?

Jekyll: WHAT?

Really: You said my NAME again.

Jekyll: No, I DIDN'T.

Really: Yes, you DID.

Jekyll: No, I DIDN'T.

Really: (*Sighing*) Oh, NEVER MIND.

(*They exit.*)

For Post-Play Pondering:

1. Why might someone want to become a new person? Have you ever wished you could?

2. Which of the following methods would you consider using to "transform" yourself: (a) plastic surgery, (b) dyeing your hair, (c) getting body parts pierced, (d) changing your name, (e) buying new clothes? Would these make you a new person? Why or why not?

3. If you could get a "makeover" that didn't involve your looks, what might you want it to include?

4. What do people mean when they say they've been "born again"? How does knowing Jesus make people "new"?

5. Have you ever known a person who changed by becoming a Christian? What kind of transformation was it? How do you think it happened?

Other Scriptures for Study:

John 3:1-8; 2 Corinthians 5:17; Ephesians 4:20-24

Bunny the Vampire Player

Topic: Fitting In
Scripture for Study:
1 Kings 11:1–11

The Scene: An underground crypt

The Simple Setup: For this spoof of *Buffy the Vampire Slayer*, set a long, strong table center stage. Place **Announcer** at an offstage microphone. **Bunny** should lie on the table before the skit starts; cover her with a sheet. **Bunny** may wear casual clothes; **Biles** should wear the more formal outfit of a school librarian. If possible, have **Biles** use a British accent. Props: Mallet (rubber or wooden) or toy hammer, and a wooden stake. Note: Don't make the stake pointed on the end, and make sure **Bunny** only pretends to pound it with the hammer.

Other Options: If you like, play a bit of the *Buffy the Vampire Slayer* TV show's theme music to lead into the skit. If you can control your lighting, darken the performing area and cast a single pool of light center stage.

The Characters:
    Announcer, dramatic and ominous
    Bunny Slippers, vampire hunter
    Mr. Biles, her mentor

▼   ▼   ▼   ▼   ▼   ▼   ▼   ▼

*(As the skit begins, we see only a sheet-covered table center stage. There appears to be something—or someone—lying under the sheet. After a few moments, **Announcer** speaks from offstage.)*

Announcer: In EVERY GENERATION there is a CHOSEN one…She ALONE will stand against the VAMPIRES, the DEMONS, and the FORCES OF DARKNESS…

*(Enter **Mr. Biles**, carrying a mallet and a wooden stake. He looks around cautiously.)*

Biles:  BUNNY? Bunny SLIPPERS? Are you HERE? Bunny, it's ME, Mr. BILES! Time to go VAMPIRE HUNTING! (**Biles** *discovers table and steps back in surprise. He looks around again.*) BUNNY? I may have FOUND one ALREADY! (*He lifts sheet, under which lies **Bunny**.*)

Bunny: HEY! Watch where you're GOING with that WOODEN STAKE, huh?

Biles: BUNNY! Why are you lying in this UNDERGROUND CRYPT? For a moment I thought you were…a VAMPIRE!

Bunny: (*Sitting up*) REALLY? GREAT! I've been PRACTICING!

Biles: Practicing WHAT?

Bunny: Acting like a VAMPIRE. Here, I'll SHOW you. (*She gets off the table, strikes a scary pose, and speaks with "Dracula" accent.*) I VANT to DRINK your BLOOD! (*Pauses, then in regular voice*) No, WAIT. Too OVER-THE-TOP. (*Strikes another scary pose, speaks in low, "cool" voice.*) It is time for me…to FEED! (*Returning to regular voice*) Yeah, that's WAY better.

Biles: Bunny, what are you DOING? You're not supposed to IMITATE vampires, you're supposed to TRACK THEM DOWN!

Bunny: Oh, Biles, you're so STUCK in a RUT. Vampires ROCK! They're MYSTERIOUS. They wear BLACK. They get to STAY OUT LATE!

Biles: But they're EVIL! They're the UNDEAD! They SUCK PEOPLE'S BLOOD and ENSLAVE THEM FOREVER!

Bunny: I didn't say they were PERFECT! They're just SO COOL!

Biles: Is it cool to BITE PEOPLE IN THE NECK? Is it cool to LIVE IN A COFFIN? Is it cool to have FANGS?

Bunny: Hey, don't KNOCK it until you've TRIED it.

Biles: Is it cool not to be able to SEE yourself in a MIRROR? Is it cool to turn to DUST if you go out in the SUN? Is it cool to have a FACE that looks like a ROTTEN GOURD?

Bunny: Biles, you are SO NEGATIVE! Maybe if you got out of that boring, old LIBRARY once in a while, you'd see that life is more than just CRUCIFIXES and GARLIC! SPEAKING of which…(*Waves hand back and forth as if to clear the air.*) they DO have ODORLESS garlic TABLETS nowadays, you know!

Biles: Bunny, you are a CHOSEN one. You are meant to be DIFFERENT from the vampires, not LIKE them! You are a vampire SLAYER!

Bunny: Not ANYMORE! I want to be a vampire PLAYER!

Biles: PLAYER? But your mission is to OVERCOME the undead, not to be overcome BY them!

Bunny: Biles, I have to FIT IN! I'm tired of STICKING OUT LIKE A SORE THUMB! I want to be like EVERYONE ELSE—like my FRIENDS!

Biles: But your friends aren't VAMPIRES. What about SANDER? What about BRILLO?

Bunny: Have you ever WATCHED those two? They're GEEKS! Besides, EVERYBODY at SCHOOL is turning into a VAMPIRE! It happens every WEEK—or haven't you NOTICED?

Biles: Bunny, I can't let you DO this. As your WATCHER, I am bound to GUIDE you in the PURSUIT and DESTRUCTION of VAMPIRES. (*Holds out hammer and stake.*) JOIN me in the quest. Do what you KNOW you MUST!

(*For a moment **Bunny** pauses, considering. Then she takes the hammer and stake.*)

Bunny: OK! (*She puts the stake to **Biles'** chest and pretends to hammer it into him.*)

Biles: AAUGGH! (*He falls as if dead.*)

Bunny: SORRY, Biles. Some things are just more IMPORTANT than keeping the world from being OVERRUN BY EVIL. (*She pats her hair and starts to leave.*) Like, for instance…my POPULARITY! (*She exits.*)

Announcer: (*From offstage*) In EVERY GENERATION there are CHOSEN ones. They ALONE will stand against the forces of DARKNESS…UNLESS, of course, they decide to…JOIN 'em.

For Post-Play Pondering:

1. Why didn't Bunny want to be a vampire slayer? Do you think she ever wanted to? If so, what changed?

2. On a scale of 1 to 10, with 10 being highest, how much do you think most kids want to "fit in"?

3. When is "fitting in" a good thing? When is it not?

4. Are Christians supposed to be "slayers" of non-Christians? If not, against whom is the "fight"? How do some Christians try to imitate non-Christians? Does this really make them more popular?

5. Do you tend to influence others more than they influence you, or is it the other way around? Is there anything about that tendency you'd like to change? If so, what?

Other Scriptures for Study:
Ezekiel 11:8-12; Luke 22:54-62; Romans 12:1-2

Contact

Topic: Inviting Others to the Group
Scripture for Study:
Luke 14:16-24

The Scene: A meeting room at church

The Simple Setup: You'll need a long table center stage, with the length running stage left to right. Place two chairs at the ends of the table and two chairs on the upstage side (facing the audience). All actors may wear casual clothes. Props: sheaf of papers for **Foster** and **Greenspan**. Note that all roles may be played by either gender.

Other Options: To further identify the characters, you could dress **Puptent** in a jumpsuit, **Foster** in a lab coat, and **Greenspan** in a suit.

The Characters:

Puptent, committee chairperson who acts like a military general
Foster, science nerd
Greenspan, uptight treasurer
Perkins, innocent new kid

(As the skit begins, all the characters except **Puptent** sit at a long table. **Foster** and **Greenspan** are at the ends of the table; **Perkins** sits in one of the upstage chairs, facing the audience. The other upstage chair is empty. **Foster** and **Greenspan** shuffle papers and look very serious; **Perkins** looks around, wide-eyed. After a few moments **Puptent** marches in, looking grim, and stands behind the empty chair.)

Puptent:	Ten…HUT! (**Foster** and **Greenspan** sit up straight.) AT EASE! (**Foster** and **Greenspan** relax somewhat.) All RIGHT! This meeting of the YOUTH GROUP OUTREACH COMMITTEE will now COME TO ORDER! Yours truly, CHAIRPERSON PUPTENT, PRESIDING! As you KNOW, we have recently received NEWS that requires IMMEDIATE ACTION. FOSTER?
Foster:	Uh, yes. It has come to our attention that…impossible as it seems…there is INTELLIGENT LIFE OUTSIDE OF OUR YOUTH GROUP.
Greenspan:	SHOCKING!
Puptent:	Yes, it IS. But as the OUTREACH COMMITTEE, it is our DUTY to determine whether it might be possible to MAKE CONTACT with these…BEINGS.
Perkins:	Um…EXCUSE me…
Puptent:	The chair recognizes…uh…Who ARE you, anyway?

Perkins: I'm PERKINS.

Puptent: YES, Perkins. What IS it?

Perkins: Well, I was thinking that we could just MEET some of these outsiders, and—

Puptent: MEET them? PREPOSTEROUS! You're NEW here, AREN'T you, Perkins?

Perkins: Well, YES, but—

Puptent: You'd better leave this to US. We've been on the outreach committee since it was FORMED! We KNOW what we're DOING!

Perkins: OK, but...

Puptent: FOSTER!

Foster: *(Startled)* Uh, YES?

Puptent: What is your RECOMMENDATION?

Foster: *(Consulting papers)* According to the extensive COMPUTER SIMULATIONS I've run, there is only ONE OPTION. In order to COMMUNICATE with these...BEINGS...we must build a MASSIVE ARRAY of POWERFUL RADIO TELESCOPES in the DESERT of NEW MEXICO.

Puptent: I SEE. And what will be the FUNCTION of these devices?

Foster: To beam electronically coded SIGNALS in the direction of these...ALIENS...in the hope that they will be able to RECEIVE and TRANSLATE them.

Perkins: TRANSLATE them? But why don't we just walk up and say—

Puptent: WALK Up? Are you MAD? Think of the DANGERS! You really ARE new here, AREN'T you, Perkins?

Perkins: But—

Puptent: FOSTER! What is the estimated COST of this massive array of radio telescopes?

Foster: Approximately ONE HUNDRED FORTY-ONE BILLION DOLLARS.

Perkins: BILLION? But all we have to DO is—

Puptent: GREENSPAN!

Greenspan: (Startled) Uh, YES?

Puptent: As our TREASURER, how do you propose we RAISE this ONE HUNDRED FORTY-ONE BILLION DOLLARS?

Greenspan: With a BAKE SALE.

Puptent: A BAKE SALE?

Greenspan: According to my projections, we can earn the necessary revenue by selling ONE CHOCOLATE BROWNIE to EVERY PERSON in a TWENTY-MILE RADIUS.

Puptent: And for WHAT PRICE would we have to sell each of these brownies?

Greenspan: Approximately TEN MILLION DOLLARS.

Puptent: That sounds a bit STEEP.

Greenspan: We could throw in a FREE CAR WASH.

Puptent: THAT should do it! Now, WHEN will we SCHEDULE this bake sale?

Perkins: EXCUSE me.

Puptent: YES, Perkins?

Perkins: Wouldn't it be EASIER and CHEAPER to make PERSONAL contact with these outsiders?

Puptent: PERSONAL contact? IMPOSSIBLE!

Foster: UNTHINKABLE!

Greenspan: UNIMAGINABLE!

Puptent: The RISKS, Perkins! The RISKS! The possibility of CONTAMINATION! The potential for EMBARRASSMENT!

Perkins: But—

Puptent: You're NEW, Perkins! You don't UNDERSTAND! You...(*Pauses to think.*) WAIT a minute.

Perkins: WHAT?

Puptent: You ARE new. How did THAT happen? Why did YOU start coming to the group?

Perkins: Well...someone in the group just CAME UP and INVITED me.

Puptent: INVITED you? PERSONALLY? At CLOSE RANGE?

Perkins: Yes...

Puptent: Without TECHNICAL SUPPORT? Without PROTECTIVE CLOTHING? Without regard for the possibility of REJECTION?

Perkins: Well...YEAH.

(**Foster** and **Greenspan** *gasp.*)

Puptent: (*Assuming a military stance*) This is a SECURITY BREACH! We have a TRAITOR among us! Someone who has PERSONALLY invited a STRANGER in order to make the rest of us LOOK BAD! (*Pauses.*) I am hereby declaring a STATE OF EMERGENCY! This meeting is ADJOURNED! We will RECONVENE in a SECURE LOCATION, the IDENTITY of which will be DELIVERED to you via TOP SECRET COURIER! That is ALL!

(**Puptent**, **Foster**, and **Greenspan** *exit.*)

Perkins: (*After a pause*) HMM. I wonder why they call it...OUTREACH?

(**Perkins** *exits.*)

For Post-Play Pondering:

1. What are three good things someone could get from joining our group?

2. What are the risks of inviting someone to our group? What's the worst that might happen? The best?

3. If you could be sure the person wouldn't reject you, would you be willing to invite someone to our group? Why or why not? If the person said "no," would that be a rejection of you personally? Explain.

4. What would be a good way to invite someone to our group? How could you phrase the invitation in fifteen words or less?

5. Who's one person you can invite to our group this week? If the person says "yes," what would you like the rest of us to do to make him or her feel welcome?

Other Scriptures for Study:

Matthew 25:37-45; John 1:43-46; Hebrews 13:2

Indexes

Topics at a Glance

Scripture Index

Group Publishing, Inc.
Attention: Product Development
P.O. Box 481
Loveland, CO 80539
Fax: (970) 669-1994

Evaluation for *Goof-Proof Skits for Youth Ministry 2*

Please help Group Publishing, Inc., continue to provide innovative and useful resources for ministry. Please take a moment to fill out this evaluation and mail or fax it to us. Thanks!

● ● ●

1. As a whole, this book has been (circle one)

not very helpful   very helpful

1   2   3   4   5   6   7   8   9   10

2. The best things about this book:

3. Ways this book could be improved:

4. Things I will change because of this book:

5. Other books I'd like to see Group publish in the future:

6. Would you be interested in field-testing future Group products and giving us your feedback? If so, please fill in the information below:

Name _____

Street Address _____

City _____ State _____ Zip _____

Phone Number _____ Date _____

Vital Ministry Resources for Pastors and Church Leaders

Reach the Back Row: Creative Approaches for High-Impact Preaching

Murray Frick with foreword by Leonard Sweet

Discover innovative approaches to connect with *every* member of your audience! You'll get new techniques for communicating the Gospel and creative ways to hook your audience. Plus, you'll discover practical ways to increase your impact and effectiveness, and get tips for turning passive listeners into active participants.

ISBN 0-7644-2126-3

New Directions for Small Group Ministry

Carl George, Paul Borthwick, Steve Sheeley, Paul Kaak, Carol Lukens and Gary Newton

Here are six practical, fresh models that help build adult small groups that *work*. It includes clear, honest evaluations of the strengths and weaknesses of each model so you'll know what's working and why—and where the pitfalls are. Essential reading for launching a small group ministry for the first time or for making your current ministry even better.

ISBN 0-7644-2137-9

Sermon-Booster Dramas

Tim Kurth

Now you can deliver powerful messages in fresh, new ways. Set up your message with memorable, easy-to-produce dramas—each just 3 minutes or less! These 25 low-prep dramas hit hot topics ranging from burnout…ethics…parenting…stress… to work…career issues and more! Your listeners will be on the edge of their seats!

ISBN 0-7644-2016-X

Bore No More! 2

This is a must-have for pastors, college/career speakers, and others who address groups! Rather than just provide illustrations to entertain audiences, the authors show readers how to *involve* audiences in the learning process. Each activity takes from two to five minutes and turns pew-sitters into willing participants, active learners, and sermon fans!

ISBN 0-7644-2109-3